# WALKS IN THE
# AUVERGNE

Titles in the Footpaths of Europe Series

**Normandy and the Seine**
**Walking through Brittany**
**Walks in Provence**
**Coastal Walks: Normandy and Brittany**
**Walking the Pyrenees**
**Walks in the Auvergne**

# WALKS IN THE
# AUVERGNE

Translated by Wendy Allatson
Translation co-ordinator: Ros Schwartz

Robertson McCarta

The publishers thank the following people for their help with this book:
Isabelle Daguin, Philippe Lambert, Vicky Hayward, Gianna Rossi, Tessa Hatts,
Eileen Cadman

First published in 1989 by

**Robertson McCarta Limited**
122 King's Cross Road.
London WC1X 9DS

in association with

**Fédération Française de Randonnée Pédestre**
8 Avenue Marceau
75008 Paris

Designed by Prue Bucknall
Production by Grahame Griffiths
Typeset by Columns of Reading
Planning Map by Robertson Merlin

Printed and bound in Hong Kong

British Library Cataloguing in Publication Data

Walks in the Auvergne — (Footpaths of Europe).
  1. France. Auvergne. Visitors' guides
  I. Allatson, Wendy   II. Series
  796–5'1'094459
  ISBN—1—85365—140—0

Every care has been taken to ensure that all the information in this book is
accurate. The publishers cannot accept any responsibility for any errors that
may appear or their consequences.

# CONTENTS

# A note from the publisher

The books in this French Walking Guide series are published in association and with the help of the Fédération Française de la Randonnée Pédestre (French ramblers' association) — generally known as the FFRP.

The FFRP is a federal organisation and is made up of regional, local and many other associations and bodies that form its constituent parts. Individual membership is through these various local organisations. The FFRP therefore acts as an umbrella organisation overseeing the waymarking of footpaths, training and the publishing of the *Topo-guides*, detailed guides to the Grande Randonnée footpaths.

There are at present about 170 Topoguides in print, compiled and written by local members of the FFRP, who are responsible for waymarking the walks — so they are well researched and accurate.

We have translated the main itinerary descriptions, amalgamating and adapting several *Topo-guides* to create new regional guides. We have retained the basic *Topo-guide* structure, indicating length and times of walks, and the Institut Géographique National (official French survey) maps overlaid with the routes.

The information contained in this guide is the latest available at the time of going to print. However, as publishers we are aware that this kind of information is continually changing and we are anxious to enhance and improve the guides as much as possible. We encourage you to send us suggestions, criticisms and those little bits of information you may wish to share with your fellow walkers. Our address is: Robertson-McCarta, 122 King's Cross Road, London WC1X 9DS.

We shall be happy to offer a free copy of any one of these books to any reader whose suggestions are subsequently incorporated into a new edition.

It is possible to create a variety of routes by referring to the walks above and to the planning map (inside the front cover). Transport and accommodation are listed in the alphabetical index at the back of the book.

# KEY

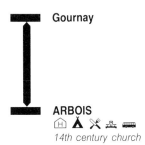

**Gournay**

This example shows that it is 7km from Gournay to Arbois, and that you can expect it to take 2 hours, 10 minutes.

**ARBOIS**
Ⓗ Å ✕ ⚒ 🚌
*14th century church*

Arbois has a variety of facilities, including hotels and buses. Hotel addresses and bus/train connections may be listed in the index at the back of the book.

A grey arrow indicates an alternative route that leaves and returns to the main route.

**Detour**

indicates a short detour off the route to a town with facilities or to an interesting sight.

---

**Symbols:**

Ⓗ hotel;
⌂ youth hostel, hut or refuge;
Å camping;
✕ restaurant;
Ⓨ cafe;

⚒ shops;
🚂 railway station;
🚌 buses;
⛴ ferry;
🛈 tourist information.

# THE FOOTPATHS OF FRANCE

## by Robin Neillands

**W**hy should you go walking in France? Well, walking is fun and as for France, Danton summed up the attractions of that country with one telling phrase: 'Every man has two countries,' he said, 'his own . . . and France.' That is certainly true in my case and I therefore consider it both a pleasure and an honour to write this general introduction to these footpath guides to France. A pleasure because walking in or through France is my favourite pastime, an honour because these excellent English language guides follow in the course set by those Topo-guides published in French by the Fédération Française pour la Randonnée Pédestre, which set a benchmark for quality that all footpath guides might follow. Besides, I believe that good things should be shared and walking in France is one of the most pleasant activities I know.

I have been walking in France for over thirty years. I began by rambling — or rather ambling — through the foothills of the Pyrenees, crossing over into Spain past the old Hospice de France, coming back over the Somport Pass in a howling blizzard, which may account for the fact that I totally missed two sets of frontier guards on both occasions. Since then I have walked in many parts of France and even from one end of it to the other, from the Channel to the Camargue, and I hope to go on walking there for many years to come.

The attractions of France are legion, but there is no finer way to see and enjoy them than on foot. France has two coasts, at least three mountain ranges — the Alps, Pyrenees and the Massif Central — an agreeable climate, a great sense of space, good food, fine wines and, believe it or not, a friendly and hospitable people. If you don't believe me, go there on foot and see for yourself. Walking in France will appeal to every kind of walker, from the day rambler to the backpacker, because above all, and in the nicest possible way, the walking in France is well organised, but those Francophiles who already know France well, will find it even more pleasureable if they explore their favourite country on foot.

### The GR system

The Grande Randonnée (GR) footpath network now consists of more than 40,000 kilometres (25,000 miles) of long-distance footpath, stretching into every part of France, forming a great sweep around Paris, probing deeply into the Alps, the Pyrenees, and the volcanic cones of the Massif Central. This network, the finest system of footpaths in Europe, is the creation of that marvellously named organisation, *la Fédération Française de Randonnée Pédestre, Comité National des Sentiers de Grande Randonnée*, which I shall abbreviate to FFRP-CNSGR. Founded in 1948, and declaring that, '*un jour de marche, huit jours de santé*,' the FFRP-CNSGR has flourished for four decades and put up the now familiar red-and-white waymarks in every corner of the country. Some of these footpaths are classic walks, like the famous GR65, *Le Chemin de St Jacques*, the ancient Pilgrim Road to Compostela, the TMB, the *Tour du Mont Blanc*, which circles the mountain through France, Switzerland and Italy, or the 600-mile long GR3, the *Sentier de la Loire*, which runs from the Ardèche to the Atlantic, to give three examples from the hundred or so GR trails available. In addition there is an abundance of GR du Pays or regional footpaths, like the *Sentier de la Haute Auvergne*, and the *Sentier Tour des Monts d'Aubrac*. A 'Tour' incidentally, is usually a circular walk. Many of these regional or provincial GR trails are charted and waymarked in red-and-yellow by local outdoor organisations such as ABRI (Association Bretonne des Relais et Itineraires) for Brittany, or CHAMINA for the Massif Central. The walker in France will soon become familiar with all these footpath networks, national, regional or local, and find them the perfect way into the heart and heartland of France. As a little bonus, the GR networks are expanding all the time, with the detours — or *varientes* — off the main route eventually linking with other GR paths or *varientes* and becoming GR trails in their own right.

Walkers will find the GR trails generally well marked and easy to follow, and they have two advantages over the footpaths commonly encountered in the UK. First, since they are laid out by local people, they are based on intricate local knowledge of the local sights. If there is a fine view, a mighty castle or a pretty village on your footpath route, your footpath through France will surely lead you to it. Secondly, all French footpaths are usually well provided with a wide range of comfortable country accommodation, and you will discover that the local people, even the farmers, are well used to walkers and greet them with a smile, a '*Bonjour*' and a '*bon route*'.

## Terrain and climate

As a glance at these guides or any Topo-guide will indicate, France has a great variety of terrain. France is twice the size of the UK and many natural features are also on a larger scale. There are three main ranges of mountains: the Alps contain the highest mountain in Europe, the Pyrenees go up to 10,000 ft, the Massif Central peaks to over 6000 ft, and there are many similar ranges with hills which overtop our highest British peak, Ben Nevis. On the other hand, the Auvergne and the Jura have marvellous open ridge walking, the Cévennes are steep and rugged, the Ardèche and parts of Provence are hot and wild, the Île de France, Normandy, Brittany and much of Western France is green and pleasant, not given to extremes. There is walking in France for every kind of walker, but given such a choice the wise walker will consider the complications of terrain and weather before setting out, and go suitably equipped.

France enjoys three types of climate: continental, oceanic and mediterranean. South of the Loire it will certainly be hot to very hot from mid-April to late September. Snow can fall on the mountains above 4,000 ft from mid-October and last until May, or even lie year-round on the tops and in couloirs; in the high hills an ice-axe is never a frill. I have used one by the Brèche de Roland in the Pyrenees in mid-June.

Wise walkers should study weather maps and forecasts carefully in the week before they leave for France, but can generally expect good, weather from May to October, and a wide variety of weather — the severity depending on the terrain — from mid-October to the late Spring.

## Accommodation

The walker in France can choose from a wide variety of accommodation with the assurance that the walker will always be welcome. This can range from country hotels to wild mountain pitches, but to stay in comfort, many walkers will travel light and overnight in the comfortable hotels of the *Logis de France* network.

*Logis de France:* The *Logis de France* is a nationwide network of small, family-run country hotels, offering comfortable accommodation and excellent food. *Logis* hotels are graded and can vary from a simple, one-star establishment, with showers and linoleum, to a four- or five-star *logis* with gastronomic menus and deep-pile carpets. All offer excellent value for money, and since there are over 5,000 scattered across the French countryside, they provide a good focus for a walking day. An annual guide to the *Logis* is available from the French Government Tourist Office, 178 Piccadilly, London W1V 0AL, Tel. (01) 491 7622.

*Gites d'Etape:* A *gîte d'étape* is best imagined as an unmanned youth hostel for outdoor folk of all ages. They lie all along the footpath networks and are usually signposted or listed in the guides. They can be very comfortable, with bunk beds, showers, a well equipped kitchen, and in some cases they have a warden, a *guardien*, who may offer meals. *Gîtes d'étape* are designed exclusively for walkers, climbers, cyclists, cross country skiers or horse-riders. A typical price (1989) would be Fr.25 for one night. *Gîtes d'étape* should not be confused with a *Gîte de France*. A *gîte* — usually signposted as '*Gîte de France*' — is a country cottage available for a holiday let, though here too, the owner may be more than willing to rent it out as overnight accommodation.

*Youth hostels:* Curiously enough, there are very few Youth Hostels in France outside the main towns. A full list of the 200 or so available can be obtained from the Youth Hostel Association (YHA), Trevelyan House, St Albans, Herts AL1 2DY.

*Pensions or cafes:* In the absence of an hotel, a *gîte d'étape* or a youth hostel, all is not lost. France has plenty of accommodation and an enquiry at the village cafe or bar will usually produce a room. The cafe/hotel may have rooms or suggest a nearby pension or a *chambre d'hôte*. Prices start at around Fr.50 for a room, rising to, say, Fr.120. (1989 estimate).

*Chambres d'hôte:* A *chambre d'hôte* is a guest room or, in English terms, a bed-and-breakfast, usually in a private house. Prices range up from about Fr.60 a night. *Chambres d'hôte* signs are now proliferating in the small villages of France and especially if you can speak a little French are an excellent way to meet the local people. Prices (1989) are from, say, Fr.70 a night for a room, not per person.

*Abris:* *Abris*, shelters or mountain huts can be found in the mountain regions, where they are often run by the *Club Alpin Français*, an association for climbers. They range from the comfortable to the primitive, are often crowded and are sometimes reserved for members. Details from the Club Alpin Français, 7 Rue la Boétie, Paris 75008, France.

*Camping:* French camp sites are graded from one to five star, but are generally very good at every level, although the facilities naturally vary from one cold tap to shops, bars and heated pools. Walkers should not be deterred by a '*Complet*' (Full) sign on the gate or office window: a walker's small tent will usually fit in somewhere. *Camping à la ferme*, or farm camping, is increasingly popular, more primitive — or less regimented — than the official sites, but widely available and perfectly adequate. Wild camping is officially not permitted in National Parks, but unofficially if you are over 1,500m away from a road, one hour's walk from a *gîte* or campsite, and where possible ask permission, you should have no trouble. French country people will always assist the walker to find a pitch.

## The law for walkers

The country people of France seem a good deal less concerned about their 'rights' than the average English farmer or landowner. I have never been ordered off land in France or greeted with anything other than friendliness . . . maybe I've been lucky. As a rule, walkers in France are free to roam over all open paths and tracks. No decent walker will leave gates open, trample crops or break down walls, and taking fruit from gardens or orchards is simply stealing. In some parts of France there are local laws about taking chestnuts, mushrooms (and snails), because these are cash crops. Signs like *Réserve de Chasse*, or *Chasse Privé* indicate that the shooting is reserved for the landowner. As a general rule, behave sensibly and you will be tolerated everywhere, even on private land.

## The country code

Walkers in France should obey the *Code du Randonneur*:

- Love and respect Nature.
- Avoid unnecessary noise.
- Destroy nothing.
- Do not leave litter.
- Do not pick flowers or plants.
- Do not disturb wildlife.
- Re-close all gates.
- Protect and preserve the habitat.
- No smoking or fires in the forests. (This rule is essential and is actively enforced by foresters and police.)
- Stay on the footpath.
- Respect and understand the country way of life and the country people.
- Think of others as you think of yourself.

## Transport

Transportation to and within France is generally excellent. There are no less than nine Channel ports: Dunkirk, Calais, Boulogne, Dieppe, Le Havre, Caen/Ouistreham, Cherbourg, Saint-Malo and Roscoff, and a surprising number of airports served by direct flights from the UK. Although some of the services are seasonal, it is often possible to fly direct to Toulouse, Poitiers, Nantes, Perpignan, Montpellier, indeed to many provincial cities, as well as to Paris and such obvious destinations as Lyon and Nice. Within France the national railway, the SNCF, still retains a nationwide network. Information, tickets and a map can be obtained from the SNCF. France also has a good country bus service and the *gare routière* is often placed just beside the railway station. Be aware though, that many French bus services only operate within the *département*, and they do not generally operate from one provincial city to the next. I cannot encourage people to hitch-hike, which is both illegal and risky, but walkers might consider a taxi for their luggage. Almost every French village has a taxi driver who will happily transport your rucksacks to the next night-stop, fifteen to twenty miles away, for Fr.50 a head or even less.

## Money

Walking in France is cheap, but banks are not common in the smaller villages, so carry a certain amount of French money and the rest in traveller's cheques or Eurocheques, which are accepted everywhere.

## Clothing and equipment

The amount of clothing and equipment you will need depends on the terrain, the length of the walk, the time of your visit, the accommodation used. Outside the mountain areas it is not necessary to take the full range of camping or backpacking gear. I once walked across France from the Channel to the Camargue along the Grande Randonnée footpaths in March, April and early May and never needed to use any of the camping gear I carried in my rucksack because I found hotels everywhere, even in quite small villages.

Essential items are:
**In summer:** light boots, a hat, shorts, suncream, lip salve, mosquito repellent, sunglasses, a sweater, a windproof cagoule, a small first-aid kit, a walking stick.
**In winter:** a change of clothing, stormproof outer garments, gaiters, hat, lip salve, a companion.
**In the mountains at any time:** large-scale maps (1:25,000), a compass, an ice-axe. In winter, add a companion and ten-point crampons.
**At any time:** a phrase book, suitable maps, a dictionary, a sense of humour.

The best guide to what to take lies in the likely weather and the terrain. France tends to be informal, so there is no need to carry a jacket or something smart for the evenings. I swear by Rohan clothing, which is light, smart and functional. The three things I would never go without are light, well-broken-in boots and several pairs of loop-stitched socks, and my walking stick.

### Health hazards
Health hazards are few. France can be hot in summer, so take a full water-bottle and refill it at every opportunity. A small first-aid kit is sensible, with plasters and 'mole-skin' for blisters, but since prevention is better than cure, loop-stitched socks and flexible boots are better. Any French chemist — a *pharmacie* — is obliged to render first-aid treatment for a small fee. These pharmacies can be found in most villages and large towns and are marked by a green cross.

Dogs are both a nuisance and a hazard. All walkers in France should carry a walking stick to fend off aggressive curs. Rabies — *la rage* — is endemic and anyone bitten must seek immediate medical advice. France also possesses two types of viper, which are common in the hill areas of the south. In fairness, although I found my walking stick indispensable, I must add that in thirty years I have never even seen a snake or a rabid dog. In case of real difficulty, dial 17 for the police and the ambulance.

### Food and wine
One of the great advantages with walking in France is that you can end the day with a good meal and not gain an ounce. French country cooking is generally excellent and good value for money, with the price of a four-course menu starting at about Fr.45. The ingredients for the mid-day picnic can be purchased from the village shops and these also sell wine. Camping-Gaz cylinders and cartridges are widely available, as is 2-star petrol for stoves. Avoid naked fires.

### Preparation
The secret of a good walk lies in making adequate preparations before you set out. It pays to be fit enough to do the daily distance at the start. Much of the necessary information is contained in this guide, but if you need more, look in guidebooks or outdoor magazines, or ask friends.

### The French
I cannot close this introduction without saying a few words about the French, not least because the walker in France is going to meet rather more French people than, say, a motorist will, and may even meet French people who have never met a foreigner before. It does help if the visitor speaks a little French, even if only enough to say '*bonjour*' and '*Merci*' and '*S'il vous plaît*'. The French tend to be formal and it pays to be

polite, to say 'hello', to shake hands. I am well aware that relations between France and England have not always been cordial over the last six hundred years or so, but I have never met with hostility of any kind in thirty years of walking through France. Indeed, I have always found that if the visitor is prepared to meet the French halfway, they will come more than halfway to greet him or her in return, and are both friendly and hospitable to the passing stranger.

As a final tip, try smiling. Even in France, or especially in France, a smile and a '*pouvez vous m'aider*?' (Can you help me?) will work wonders. That's my last bit of advice, and all I need do now is wish you '*Bonne Route*' and good walking in France.

# WALKS IN THE AUVERGNE

Robin Neillands

Although France is well supplied with excellent walking areas, few — indeed none that I can think of — can match the diversity of terrain, the spectacular scenery and the great sense of space that forms part of the wonderful Auvergne. Having walked across the Auvergne on my walk from the Channel to the Camargue, I remember the footpaths through the Auvergne as the most perfect section of the entire route, and the Auvergne is the one region of France that I would recommend unhesitatingly both to experienced walkers who have never walked in France, and to committed Francophiles who have yet to try walking in France.

The reasons for this partiality are quite simple. Experienced walkers will find in the Auvergne a variety of terrain suitable for every kind of walking, on high, 1,800 metre peaks, on ridges, across lake-dotted, grassy plains and barren plateaux, on a series of curious cones, the relics of long extinct volcanoes, all in beautiful country which is virtually empty of people. The Auvergne is ideal for backpacking, for long-distance walks from village to village, for circular tours, or simply for day-walking out into the country from small villages and pleasant towns.

Those who already know France well can only really get to know the Auvergne if they travel through it on foot. Indeed, there are many parts of this beautiful province that cannot be reached in any other way — Vassivière, the lake at Montcinyre near Egliseneuve-d'Entraigues, the top of the Plomb de Cantal, the great Planèze, or plateau between Lioran and Saint-Flour, the rolling country of the beautiful Aubrac, all can only be explored on foot. The Auvergne lies well off the too-well-trodden tourist routes, and is therefore very French, a land of castles, small villages, home of a dour but friendly people, the Auvergnats.

## Getting there
Access to the Auvergne is best achieved by train, with Saint-Flour, Clermont-Ferrand and Le Puy as the main terminals, plus a score of little stations that lie on the Paris–Nimes main line. There are a number of branch lines, feeding La Bourboule, Le Mont Dore, Ruines, Lugarde, Lioran.

Bus services tend to operate within the *départements*, Puy de Dôme, Cantal, Lozère, but details can be obtained from the French Rail office in London, or from the French Government Tourist Office. It is also worth remembering that since in car-terms, walking distances are short, it may be well worth while to hire a taxi for the trip to the start of the walk and back from the finish.

## Accommodation
There is no lack of accommodation in the Auvergne, much of it in small hotels. Even the smallest village seems to have at least one hotel, and to these one can add *gîtes d'étape*, *chambres d'hôte*, and a great number and variety of camp sites.

## Climate
The weather walkers will encounter in the Auvergne wil vary with the terrain and the altitude. This is a downhill and cross-country skiing area in winter, with Mont Dore as

just one popular resort, and the winter can begin early, by mid-October, and leave deep snow on the hilltops until May. I have even met a blizzard on the Aubrac plateau in June, but in general this area will be fairly hot, at 30° C or more in the summer months.

Therefore, during these summer months — May to October — the walker must be prepared for high temperatures and should be careful to carry water and replenish supplies, drinking deeply and refilling the water-bottle at every opportunity. Fortunately there are plenty of streams and stand-pipes, though purifying tablets might be advisable if using water from such sources.

## Terrain

The Auvergne terrain is extremely varied, but tends to be hilly or mountainous, with the main peaks and ranges, the Monts Dore and the Monts du Cantal, rising steeply to over the 1,800m (6,000 ft) mark. Generally, this is an area that will appeal to hill-walkers and backpackers, who should be in good physical condition before they start, if they are to enjoy all the Auvergne has to offer. That said, there are excellent day-walking areas and many pleasant valleys, and even the footpath along the Chaîne des Volcans lies in easy reach of places like Orcival.

## Clothing and equipment

See notes above on climate and terrain. What you carry will depend on where and when you go, but in winter or summer cater for extremes, while allowing for changes. For example, in summer take shorts and light clothes, which you will certainly need, but pack rain gear and a sweater, which might well come in handy. Suncream and lip salve will prove useful in any season, boots are essential, maps should be of the 1:50,000 or 1:25,000 scale, and a compass should be carried. An ice-axe and boots are recommended for anyone walking in the mountain areas or at either end of the summer season when snow or ice may be encountered.

## Hazards

The Auvergne is a large and rather desolate depopulated region, so a good companion might be advisable. Be wary of the Auvergne cattle, which are half wild, and do carry a stick to fend off farmyard dogs. Their bark may well be worse than their bite, but why take chances?

## Food and drink

The Auvergne is not one of the great gastronomique areas of France, but the general standard of country cooking is very high. The food tends to be of the soups and stews variety, ideal for walkers, and there are good, low-priced 'menus' available at prices from (circa 1988) Fr.45 for four courses. The best of the local wine comes from Saint Porçain.

## Where to go

The Auvergne is full of good walking, but from my experience there are three areas which demand particular attention, since they offer terrain which is unlike anything available in the United Kingdom. The first of these is the Chaîne des Puys, west of Clermont-Ferrand, in the Monts Dore. These 'puys' are the cones of extinct volcanoes, some intact, some shattered by eruptions, many containing deep blue lakes. There are over eighty of these extinct volcanoes and they have created a landscape of rolling, rounded hills, which is both extremely beautiful and almost unearthly. The largest of these hills is the Puy de Dôme itself, which can be seen from Clermont-Ferrand, and the entire chain is straddled by the GR4-441 footpath.

My second choice would be a week's walking south from Orcival across the Monts Dore to Besse, a ski resort in winter, and then south-east to Saint-Flour. This offers an unmatched variety of scenery and terrain, with two 1,800 metre ranges to climb above Le Mont Dore and Lioran, the great Planèze plateau between the Plomb de Cantal and Saint Flour, and, south of the Monts Dore, beautiful moorland country threaded with trout streams, from Besse to Condat. In the Spring this is an enchanted land where whole meadows are ablaze with daffodils.

Finally, for a little day-walking, I would recommend a base at Orcival, Lioran or Saint-Flour. All of these are attractive places in their own right and Orcival is a famous place, with a marvellous Romanesque church and many good *Logis* hotels. From Orcival there are good walks in every direction, past lakes and volcanoes to Mont Dore, out to the castle at Cordes, even on a good day over the hills to Beaune-le-Froid and down to the lake at Chambon. At Lioran the Monts de Cantal lie all about, so this is a good base for those who like hill-walking . . . and there is a cable car to take travellers up to the Plomb de Cantal if they prefer to leave out the hard part. Saint-Flour is a very fine town and apart from the main GRs can also offer a GR du Pays, a regional footpath, the Sentier de la Haute-Auvergne. One beautiful walk lies down this GR du Pays to the magnificent castle at Alleuze, even as far as the little village of St Juéry, which is just in Lozère.

From Saint Flour it is also possible to walk east into the country of the Margaride, a heavily forested area with magnificent walking available across rolling hills. Saint Flour is also a railway junction, so it is possible to take a train out from there to the Aubrac, or east towards Lioran, and do more walking from there.

Those who have the time would be well advised to follow the GR4 across the Auvergne to the Puy de Dôme all the way from Langogne. This would be both an experience and a challenge, but it lies well within the grasp of any competent hill-walker, for there is no need to carry heavy loads or make great distances in any one day. This path will take the walker through the finest walking country in France, and leave him or her at the end of it, secure in the knowledge that there is plenty more walking like this, down in the beautiful Auvergne.

# WALK 1

## LANGOGNE
🏠 ⛺ 🍴 �"&" ☕

*915 m*
*11th century church, 18th century covered market*

13Km
4:30

**La Tuilerie**

**Bessettes**

Take the Rue Haute which leads from the covered market, the corn exchange, up to the district of Les Lombards. You go through a recently built residential area, past the hospital, and come to the crossroads at La Tuilerie. A new section of the GR4, which avoids the D34, has been marked out between La Tuilerie and the Croix de Paillères, following the edge of the stretch of water at Naussac and passing through Le Reynaldès. This route crosses marshy valley bottoms which become impassable in wet weather. In this event, follow the alternative route.

**Alternative route:** La Tuilerie to Bessettes (GR4A). From the crossroads at La Tuilerie, turn off to the left in the direction of Rocles and follow the road (D34) for 3 kilometres. In places you can walk on the grass verges rather than on the road. You come to a bridge, the Pont du Bonjour, which you cross and, after 600 metres, turn right onto the path to Masallet. To the right of the farm, a narrow pathway bordered by old walls slopes up gently north-west and, 500 metres further on, crosses a dirt track. Turn left onto it and follow it for 700 metres until you come back to the D34. Here you turn right and walk northwards for 10 metres before turning left along a little road which comes out onto the lane leading to Rocles. Turn right at the intersection and walk northwards to Les Combelles where you again cross the D34. Straight ahead of you, another little road leads northwards, past two wayside crosses, the Croix de Besse and then the Croix de Paillères. From there, continue along a wide granite pathway and, 500 metres downhill, turn left onto a grassy pathway. Here you rejoin the GR4 at Bessettes.

The GR4 pathway passes through Bessettes and carries on towards the north-west, through Le Grand Champ to Florac (see map ref k). Here, take the road to Auroux and, 200 metres after the Croix de Florac, take a short cut leading straight ahead, which brings you back onto the road just outside Auroux.

## AUROUX

⌂ Ⓗ ⛺ ⛲

*1,000 m*
*market town*

12Km
3:30

*The quiet road linking*
*Auroux to Grandrieu via*
*L'Herm, Les Salles, Sainte-*
*Colombe-de-Montauroux*
*and Florensac, is an old royal*
*road which offers some very*
*beautiful views eastwards to*
*the Gorges de l'Allier and*
*the Monts du Velay. There*
*are several short cuts, some*
*of which are not shown on*
*the IGN 1/50.000 map.*

## GRANDRIEU

⌂ Ⓗ ⛲ 🚌

*1,150 m*
*Centre for extraction of*
*uranium ore.*
*13th century church*
*Junction with GR4*

6Km
1:45

**Alternative route:** Auroux to Grandrieu (GR4). To leave Auroux, follow the road down to the mill and across a stream, the Chapeauroux, then follow its left bank upstream as far as the road to Grandrieu. Turn left off the road and follow the western edge of a wood, the Bois du Puy, to the plateau. The path crosses a road (D226), turning gradually north-west and crossing a stream, the Bouret, at 1182 metres, before coming to the hamlet of Bellelande. Continue along a small road to Aubespeyre, and then to La Fage, via the 1239 metre mark, and to Le Masel via the 1161 metre mark. From Le Masel, the path brings you out onto the road from Grandrieu to Auroux and the GR4 near the 1159 metre mark. Cross the road, take the 'Roman' bridge over the River Grandrieu and continue up to the church.

You leave Auroux, past the mill and following the left bank of the Chapeauroux upstream as far as the road. The path goes on to L'Herm above the road. Just before Les Salles there is a short cut across the ravine (not marked on the map). At Sainte-Colombe the GR4 meets the GR412, which runs through the Gorges de l'Allier; the two GRs run together for a short distance until they reach the hamlet of Espinousette. The GR412 then runs southwards towards the hamlet of La Brugère and joins the alternative route, the GR4A, at the village of La Fage. Another short cut leaves the road just outside Espinousette, coming back onto it half way to Florensac. After Bouchet-Fraisse, not far from the wayside cross situated at 1159 metres, a path leads down to the right, crosses the 'Roman' bridge over the River Grandrieu and continues up to the church.

Take the N585 which leads west out of the village. After the bridge over a stream called the Bataille, climb north-west to the hamlet of Les Mèdes and from there take a short cut which cuts across a bend in the road. You pass a wayside cross, the Croix du Chapel, at 1188 metres, and come to the hamlet of La Bataille. From there, you continue north-west until you reach a farm, the Ferme de la Brugerette, and the village of Saint-Paul-le-Froid.

**Saint-Paul-le-Froid**
*1,280 m*

12Km
3:30

Leave the village, walking west, and take the path leading north-west, which runs down to the road (D59) and on to the hamlet of Les Martines. The path continues north-west across the River Ance and then follows its left bank at a distance until it crosses a stream, the Ruisseau des Barrières. (An alternative route, marked with dotted lines on the maps, leads off to the north, passing via Brenac, the Buron du Sauvage and the Gîte du Sauvage.) After 700 metres, take the cart track to the left, which leads westwards across Les Barrières and comes out on the D7 a little to the west of the 1432 metre mark on the ridge of La Margeride. Follow the road to the south-west and 400 metres further on you will come to the junction with the GR43, called the 'Draille de la Margeride' — *draille* means footpath — southwards to the Cabane des Bouviers (Herdsmen's Hut). A little further on, turn left (south), and then, after 150 metres, right (west). This brings you back onto the D7, which you follow to Sainte-Eulalie.

**Sainte-Eulalie**
*1,240 m*

Take the path leading north-west from the village to La Roche. The path is not as straight as it is shown on the map: it bears off to the 1291 metre mark and then runs back down again, and is not easily seen. At a beech copse, you come to a dirt track, which runs alongside an enclosure. After crossing a stream, the Limagnole, you come to the village of La Roche.

**LA ROCHE**

Leave it, walking west, and go as far as the bend of the N587, which is at an altitude of 1,184 metres. Take a dirt track, which leads off from the centre of the bend and slopes gently down to the junction with the GR65, which comes in from the right (north-east) from the village of Sauges. The two GRs run together for 300 metres and then separate after crossing a stream, the Gazamas, by way of an old bridge, at an altitude of 1155 metres, with the GR65 continuing south-west towards Saint-Alban-sur-Limagnole. The GR4 leaves the path to lead north-west into an enclosed pine-wood, where the track, which is difficult to follow at first, becomes clearly defined; this is the Chemin des Loups, or Pathway of the Wolves. You will cross a path from Lajo to Ferluc, leading to a sawmill, and then a path from Lajo to Le Marlet, before coming out on the path from Lajo to L'Estival. At this junction, you turn left and follow the path until you come to a large stone surmounted by a cross. At the far end of L'Estival, you will cross the road leading to Le Marlet; here, take the path running north-west. After crossing a stream, the Mialanette, you come to La Vialette. Go northwards through the hamlet and take a path running north-west to the 1175 metre mark, where you cross a road (D14) and continue through a wood, the Bois de Montruffet. Cross the path leading from Mialanes to L'Estivalet and continue along a path not shown on the map. When you come to the path from Les Ducs to L'Estivalet, turn left along it. From L'Estivalet, follow the lane south for 400 metres and then take a short cut off to the left, running north of Truc de la Fage. When you come back onto the road, turn left along it for 250 metres and then take the path which follows the boundary of the communes, bringing you out on the D14. Follow the road south-east to its junction with the D4, where you turn right to Malzieu-Ville.

17.5Km
5

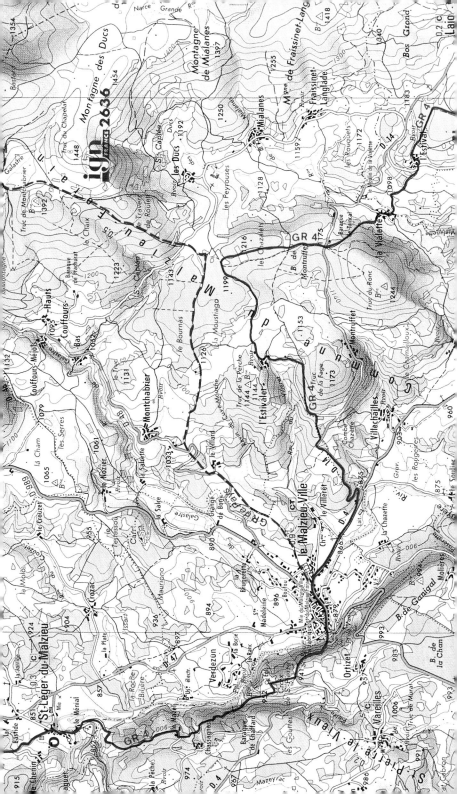

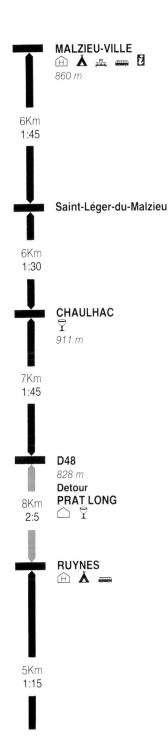

**MALZIEU-VILLE**
*860 m*

6Km
1:45

**Saint-Léger-du-Malzieu**

6Km
1:30

**CHAULHAC**
*911 m*

7Km
1:45

**D48**
*828 m*
**Detour**
**PRAT LONG**

8Km
2:5

**RUYNES**

5Km
1:15

Cross the bridge over the River Truyère and take a path directly opposite, which soon brings you out onto the D4. Carry on up the road until you come to a wayside cross, the Croix de Saint-Pierre, at 941 metres; a little further north, you come to a church, l'Eglise de Saint-Pierre. There, the path twists briefly to the south-east and then turns north again, passing through Lę Mazel to join the D75 at Le Ménial. Here, it crosses the River Truyère, before going on to Saint-Léger-du-Malzieu.

Take the D147 northwards in the direction of the cemetery and follow it for about 1 kilometre. An old pathway off to the left leads up to La Vessière, where it crosses the D147 in the hamlet and continues across La Chan de Nozerolles to meet the D8 just outside Chaulhac.

Follow the D8 to the hamlet of Paladines, after which the GR4 runs steeply down into a valley where there is a stream, the Chazette, and then climbs to La Besse. Carry straight on northwards until you come to Lusclade and the D50; turn left on to it and follow it north-west for 500 metres. A short cut takes you left off the road, across a stream, the Encaillou, and a new section of pathway branches off from the old one to meet the D48.

**Alternative route:** junction with D48 to Rastel stream, via Ruynes. Follow the D48 north for about 500 metres and then turn left along the D50 for several metres. Take a path which climbs northwards to Chauliaguet from where a path continues northwards to Ruynes-en-Margeride.

From here, follow the D13 to the railway line. You cross the line to the north of the station and then the road which runs parallel to it. A little path opposite takes you back onto the GR4 and to the D350 (807 metres) at a little bridge over a stream, the Rastel. The GR4 crosses the D48 and meets the D50 at the Baraque des Chaliers hut. Follow the D50 to the left for 400 metres and, as you go into a pine wood, take the path on the left leading down to a mill on a stream, the Ruisseau de la Roche. The path then climbs to the north-west, crossing the D13 at a level crossing next to a

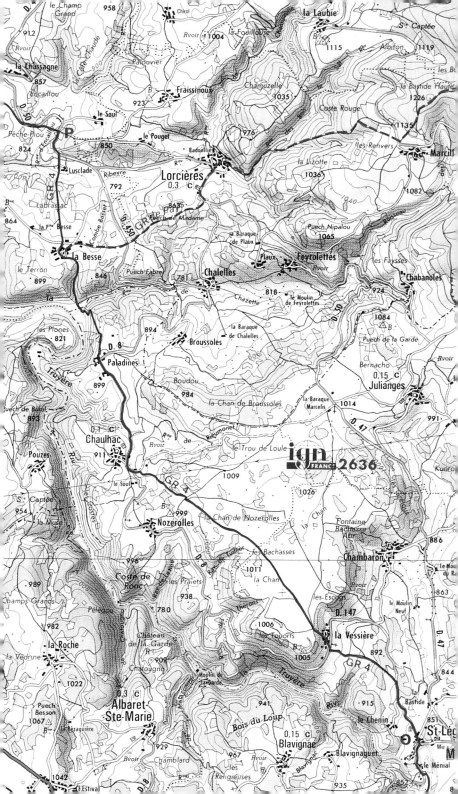

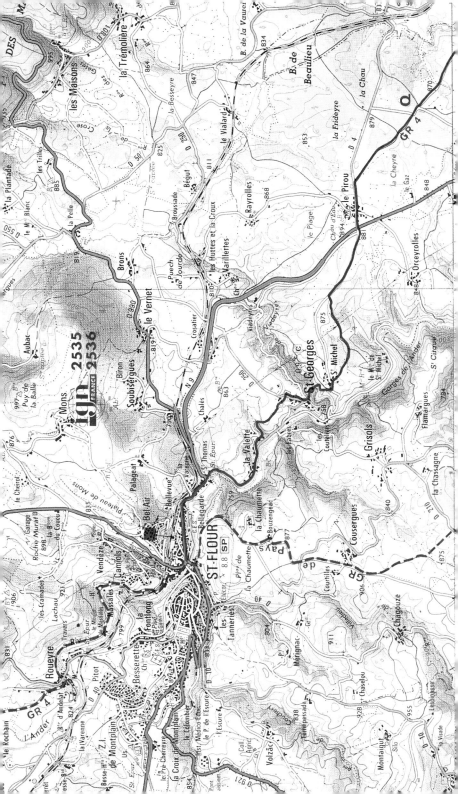

**GARE DE RUYNES**

4Km
1

**SAINT-GEORGES**
N9

7Km
1:45

**SAINT-FLOUR**

*880 m*
*Former capital of the upper*
*Auvergne, Saint-Flour is a*
*picturesque town perched*
*on basalt rock with old*
*houses clustered round an*
*austere Gothic cathedral and*
*a large cattle market.*
*Places of interest: former*
*bishop's palace housing*
*Musée de la Haute*
*Auvergne, a museum of*
*folklore, religious art and*
*archeology; consular house*
*with 16th century façade,*
*housing Musée A. Douët,*
*with exhibits of weaponry*
*and ancient furniture.*

hamlet called Signalause. Cross the railway line, making sure you close the barrier securely behind you, then follow it northwards to the Gare de Ruynes.

Opposite the station, follow the path leading westwards down to the little bridge over a stream, the Rastel. Before you come to the bridge, the GR4A comes in from the right. Cross the bridge and climb up onto a path to the right of the road. It leads north-west, bringing you out onto the D4, where you turn left towards Pirou and, beyond that, the N9.

Cross the N9, following the D4, then take a clearly marked route to Saint-Michel, a hamlet in the valley of the River Ander, and the village of Saint-Georges. The GR4 follows the left bank of the Ander up the valley and passes through the hamlets of La Valette and Saint-Thomas. Here you come back onto the N9; turn left for the town of Saint-Flour.

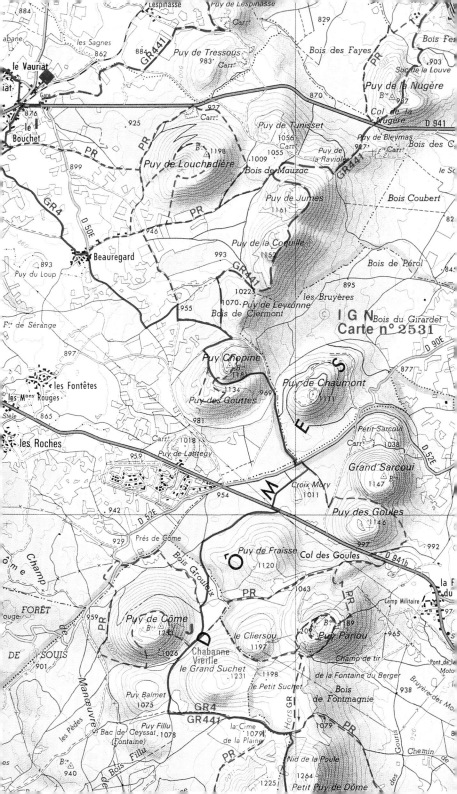

# WALK 2

The walk described in this part of the guide runs from north to south across the mountains and volcanic plateaux of the Auvergne by way of the highest and most impressive summits of the Massif Central — the Puy de Dôme (1,464 metres), the Puy de Sancy (1,885 metres), the Puy Mary (1,783 metres) and the Plomb du Cantal (1,855 metres).

(The word *puy* itself means mountain or height and originated in the Middle Ages from the Latin *podium*, meaning plinth or mound; today it refers specifically to the summits of the volcanic mountains of the Massif Central).

All these lie within the *Parc Naturel Régional des Volcans d'Auvergne*, a regional nature reserve which protects the most amazing natural museum of volcanic forms. The Chaîne des Dômes consists of some 80 volcanoes which, because they are relatively young (between 4,000 and 8,000 years old) have not been seriously damaged by erosion. Lined up on a platform 900 metres high and 30 kilometres in length is an amazing series: on the one hand forms like those of Stromboli and Pelée, on the other the Cheires, lava flows characteristic of the Auvergne, which are in some places cultivated, in others strewn with rocks and suitable only for grazing sheep. Dotted here and there, like oases, are hamlets which take their names from the sources, or *fonts*, few and far between, which provide their water supply.

In the Massif du Sancy, the austere beauty of the Auvergne is adorned with jewel-like glacial and volcanic lakes and some of the most beautiful Romanesque churches of the region, which nestle in an almost Alpine landscape cut by deep valleys with gushing thermal springs, like those of La Bourboule and Le Mont-Dore.

Towards the south, the footpath crosses the glaciers of the Artense, a creased and seamed landscape marked by the black steeples of the sleepy but welcoming villages of Egliseneuve, Condat, Lugarde and Saint-Saturnin. And then comes the long climb between earth and sky, up to the Plateau du Limon, an abstract landscape brought to life by the brown and mahogany tones of the herds of Salers cattle, which graze here. Here you reach heights of over 1,600 metres.

The Monts du Cantal cover four times the surface area of their neighbours, the Monts Dore: 2,700 square kilometres as opposed to 600 square kilometres. They are the remains of a very old volcano, 70 kilometres in diameter, which was broken up by glacial erosion. Although once covered with beautiful forests, the Massif du Cantal, like its neighbour the Sancy, has suffered from deforestation: nothing hinders the view of the landscape from the top of the surrounding ridges. Further on, these ridges flatten out, giving way to triangular plateaux. And then you come to the volcanic plateau of Saint-Flour, formerly one of the important cereal growing areas of the Auvergne,and finally to Saint-Flour itself, whose dark and lofty outline epitomises for many a tourist the characteristic image of the Auvergne. The creation of the Parc Naturel Régional des Volcans d'Auvergne, by the Conseil Régional of the Auvergne, finally took place on the 25th October 1977.

**Le Vauriat**
*(see map ref I)*

The GR4 crosses the railway line at the level crossing and then parts company with the GR441, which continues straight ahead towards Volvic. Turn right along the road to Le Bouchet; just before you get there, take a path off to the left and then the second path on the right, which takes you around Le Bouchet. At

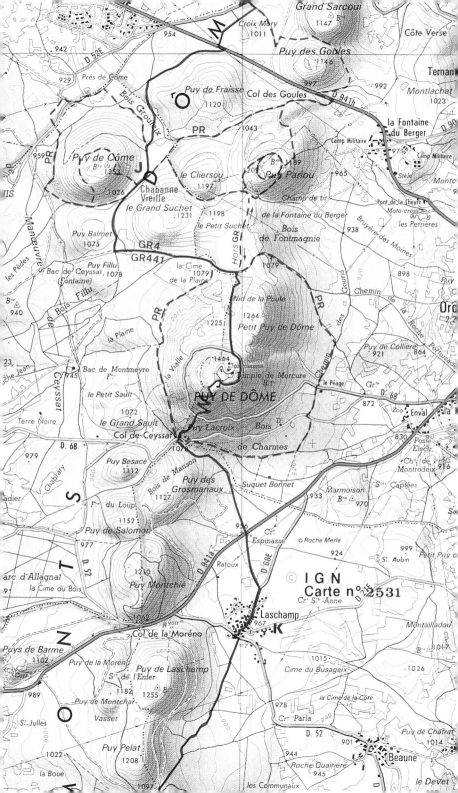

**5.5Km**
**1:30**

the junction with a PR route marked in yellow, turn left along the path bordered by low stone walls. When you come to a fork, carry on to the right until you come to a pathway covered with loose stones, which leads off to the left into the hamlet of Beauregard. Go through the hamlet and turn right along a tree-lined farm track. Follow it for 1.5 kilometres until you come to a grassy junction. Here you turn left and after 500 metres come out onto a pathway at the 955 metre mark. Turn right along the pathway and follow it southwards for 200 metres, then take a forest path off to the left, leading up to the junction with the GR441.

**Junction with the GR441**
*1,000 m*
*Situated to the north of the Puy Chopine; here the GR441 rejoins the GR4 to follow the same route as far as Pessade.*

The GRs come out onto a broad forest path. Follow it to the right for 400 metres, then climb left along the track in the hollow between the Puy Chopine and the Puy des Gouttes.

*Puy Chopine with its enormous lava peak, is the volcano in the Auvergne most closely comparable to Mount Pelée. The term Pelean volcano suits it exactly.*

**6Km**
**1:40**

The path leads down through the trees on the other side and comes out onto a wide path at the foot of the *puys*. Follow this to the right for 200 metres and then turn off left along a rutted pathway. You will cross a road (D52E) and, after following the path through the woods for 100 metres, turn right. The path brings you out onto another road (D941B) just next to a high voltage electricity cable. Turn left onto the road, walk along it for 50 metres and then turn right into the trees at an electricity pylon. After walking for 1 kilometre, you will reach a junction; here turn left then carry on south until you reach a large clearing at a spot known as Chabanne-Vieille.

**Chabanne-Vieille**
*(see map ref J)*
*1,000 m*
**Detour** *50 mins*
**LA FONTAINE DU BERGER**
✕ ♉
*via the Col de Goules and D941B eastwards*
*2 km*
**ORCINES**
Ⓗ

**6Km**
**2**

At Chabanne-Vieille, bear left through the hazel trees along the small valley between the Puy de Côme and the Puy du Grand Suchet. After the Puy Balmet and opposite the Puy Fillu, you come out into a vast open area (part of the extensive damage in this area of the forest caused by the storm of November 1982). Turn left along the path which climbs gently up to the Cime de la Plaine, a large pass at the foot of the Puy de Dôme.

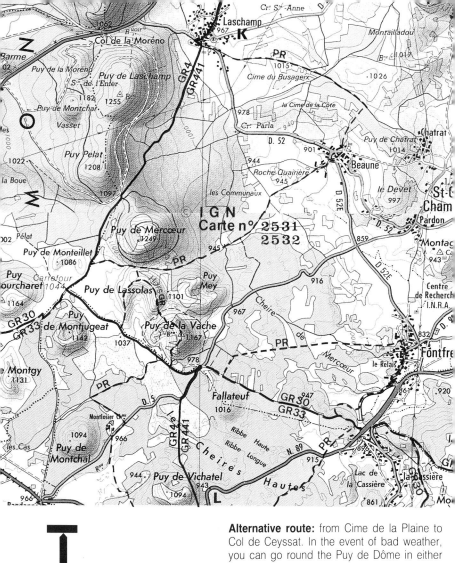

**Alternative route:** from Cime de la Plaine to Col de Ceyssat. In the event of bad weather, you can go round the Puy de Dôme in either direction. A PR route marked in yellow does a full circuit, marked in a clockwise direction. You rejoin the GR4 to the south of the Puy at the Col de Ceyssat.

The GRs GR4 and GR41 continue to run together, following a sunken track southwards to the foot of the Puy de Dôme. Climb up to the right through the trees and then across a hollow of volcanic ash (*pozzuolana*) to a crater, the Nid de la Poule. Skirt round to the right of the crater and then take a well defined track leading to the top of the Puy which brings you onto the access road to the summit. Continue along the grass verge (pedestrians are not allowed on the road) and you will come out at the parking platform.

## PUY DE DÔME SUMMIT
🏠 ✕ ⛾ 🅿
*1,464 m*
*Well laid out footpaths and panoramic maps. Fine views. Ruins of temple of Mercury. Circuit of summit area recommended.*

1.5Km
0:30

The path follows the old Roman way down from the summit, starting south of the car park near 'le dôme,' the big hotel-restaurant. It cuts across the access road half-way down and from there continues to the Col de Ceyssat.

## COL DE CEYSSAT
✕
*1,078 m*
*Junction with the PR route circuiting base of Puy de Dôme (see alternative route, above).*

3.5Km
0:50

Go down to the road, follow it to the left for 50 metres and then turn right onto the footpath leading through a beech grove where you may find recently felled trees. Bear left along the edge of a coniferous wood until you come to a road (D941A). Cross the road and take a pathway opposite, near a wayside cross, which runs south-east and brings you out onto the road (D68E) leading past the cemetery into Laschamp.

## LASCHAMP
⌂ ⛾
*(see map ref k)*
*967 m*

4Km
1

Just after the gîte, which is on the village square, turn left between the houses, cross a road and then go up the main road (D52) opposite, from where there is a departure point for a PR route marked in yellow. Follow a path leading south-west across the meadows and up into the forest. When you come to a big junction of several pathways, carry straight on, passing the Puy de Mercoeur, where you will see an antenna, on your left. The PR route from Laschamp joins the path from the left on the edge of a vast moor which lies between the surrounding Puys.

**Detour**
**Crater of Puy de Lassolas**
*By PR*

**Detour**, see left. Follow the yellow markings to the Col de Lassolas, not shown on the maps, which lies between the·Puy de Lassolas and the Puy de Mercoeur. From here you can reach the upper rim of the crater of Lassolas. You can then either follow its western rim, which brings you back down to the GR, or carry on to the rim of the crater of the Puy de la Vache before coming back down to the GR close to the junction with the D5. The GR4 and the GR441 carry on running south-west until they reach a junction at the 1044 metre mark.

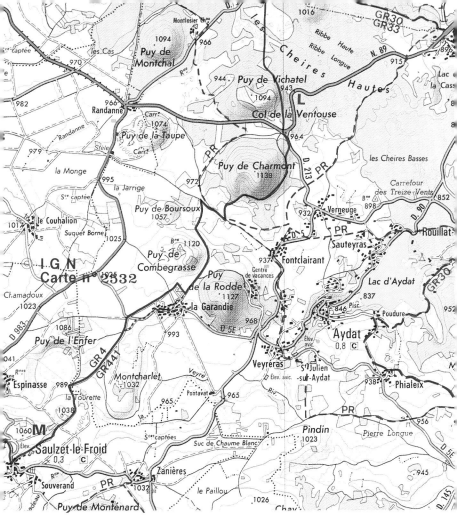

### Grand Carrefour

*1,044 m mark; junction with the GR30 and the GR33, indicated by a signpost.*

2.5Km
0:35

### Detour, *30 mins,*
### CHÂTEAU DE
### MONTLOSIER
△ 🛈

*headquarters of Parc Naturel Régional des Volcans d'Auvergne.*
*By PR.*

At the junction, turn left, south-east, past the breached craters of the Puy de Lassolas and the Puy de la Vache.

**Detour**, see left. Turn right off the GR, following the dotted line on the map. From the château, you can take an alternative route along a PR marked in green, which takes you across the N89 to the west of the Col de la Ventouse and Puy de Charmont, rejoining the GR4 shortly before La Garandie.

The GRs continue towards the south-east, going into a wood and coming out onto the D5.

**D5**
*978 m*

2Km
0:30

**Col de la Ventouse**
*(see map ref L)*
**Detour** *2 km (N89)*
**RANDANNE**

4Km
1

**Detour** *1 hour*
**LAC D'AYDAT**

*(PR) from junction south of Puy de Charmont*

**LA GARANDIE**

*1,000 m*

*The Narse d'Espinasse, produced by the filling in of a lake in a crater, has retained flora and fauna characteristic of marshland. At its northern end, at the foot of the Puy de l'Enfer, there are bullrushes, sedge, marsh horsetail and woodrushes, whilst higher up you will find spruce and broom.*

4Km
1

Here you stay on the road, while the GR30 and the GR33 carry on south-east. Where the GR4 and the GR441 meet the D5, turn right along the road for 200 metres and then take a footpath off to the left. This will take you back into the trees and across the lava flows of the Cheires to the Col de la Ventouse.

The GRs cross the central platform of the Col and make their way towards the D123, where they immediately turn right onto a broad forest path leading up through the woods and round the eastern side of the Puy de Charmont (1,138 metres). You come down on the southern side of the Puy. Turn right along a broad pathway for 300 metres and you will come to the junction with PR coming from the Puy de la Vache and the Château de Montlosier.

The GRs turn left across the moor and follow a path up to the pass between the Puy de Combegrasse (1,120 metres) on the right and the Puy de la Rodde (1,127 metres) on the left, from where there are views across to the Massif du Sancy in one direction and part of the Chaîne des Monts Dôme in the other. The GRs lead down to just outside the hamlet of La Garandie.

The GRs turn right, north, and skirt round to the west of La Garandie until they come to the D5E. You cross the road and pass some drinking troughs, which are the starting point for a PR route marked in blue. Follow the path leading down to the south-west. After 1 kilometre it crosses a stream, the Veyre, at the Narse d'Espinasse.

When you reach the 989 metre mark, go up a slight incline and past a small outcrop, known as La Tourette, on your left. Carry on to Saulzet-le-Froid.

## SAULZET-LE-FROID
(see map ref M)
1,034 m

3Km
0:45

## PESSADE
1,172 m

In Saulzet-le-Froid, the GRs turn right along the D74 for 500 metres. After a bend in the road below a wayside cross, the Croix Saint-Roch, turn along the path leading upwards along the edge of a cultivated field. It crosses an area of large meadows and carries straight on to Pessade.

The GR441 leaves the GR4, turning right, northwards, towards the Lac de Servières.

The path from Pessade used to be the road to the spa town of Mont-Dore, known as the 'royal road', and was much used in the 18th century, notably by the Marquise de Sevigne.

The GR4 passes a public washing-place and follows a pathway, climbing south-west. You go through the gates and follow the path which loops upwards to the Puy de la Vedrine (1,311 metres). The path passes near a wood, the Bois de Passade, to the right of the Puy de Baladou (1,455 metres), and continues in the same south-southwesterly direction, more or less on the level, coming out on the D996 (see map ref N). Turn left onto the road and follow it for 500 metres towards the Col de la Croix Morand.

**Col de la Croix-Morand**
*1,401 m*

As the GR4 approaches the huts on the Col, it climbs steeply up the slope to the right, following the chairlift, to the summit of the Puy de la Tache (1,629 metres). Here, you take a clearly defined pathway which follows the watershed due south via the Puy de Monne (1,692 metres), the Puy de Barbier (1,702 metres) and the Puy de l'Angle (1,738 metres). It then leads quite steeply down to a pass at the foot of the Puy de Mareilh and continues down to the D36, where you come out near an enclosure a few metres from the Col de la Croix Saint-Robert.

**Col de la Croix Saint-Robert**
*(see map ref N')*
**Detour**, *40 mins*
**Le Mont-Dore**
*1,050 m*

**Alternative route** (GR4E) Col de la Croix-Morand to Col de la Cabane du Sancy (see map ref O). This route, marked in red and white, avoids the whole of the northern and eastern watershed of the Massif du Sancy, and can be used in the event of bad weather or to stop off at Le Mont-Dore. It is also possible to leave the GR4 and reach Le Mont-Dore from the Col de la Croix Saint-Robert, 2 hours walk from the Col de la Croix-Morand.

Just before your reach the D996, take a path leading down through pasture which gradually departs from the road. It bears left and comes to a farm, the Ferme de la Tache. Take the road leading from the farm, cross the D983 and follow the path down to a waterfall, the Cascade du Rossignolet. Bear left to another waterfall, the Cascade du Queureuilh, and carry on to the hamlet of Prends-Toi-Garde. The GR4E turns due south and comes out onto the D996 in the Queureuilh district of Le Mont-Dore. Turn left into the centre of the town.

**Detour**, see left. Turn right along a PR route marked in green, and follow it (in the opposite direction to the markings) via the Creux des Boeufs. You come out directly above a waterfall, the Grande Cascade, from where a path leads down into Mont-Dore.

**LE MONT-DORE**

*1,050 m*

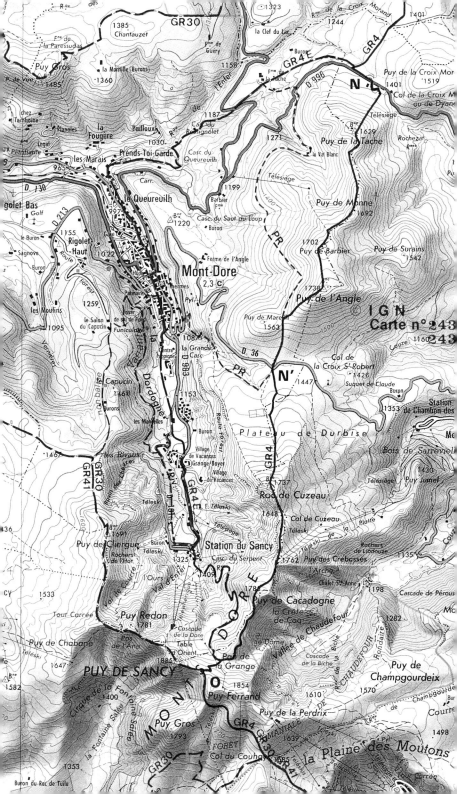

*Departure point for marked walking routes.*

From Le Mont-Dore there are three possibilities for rejoining the GR4 at Col de la Cabane du Sancy.

**Alternative route 1:** GR4E via Station de Sancy to Col de la Cabane du Sancy. Leave Le Mont-Dore, walking south and take the GR4E which closely follows the direction of the River Dordogne. It climbs upwards, using sections of the more westerly of two roads, the D101, leading to the Station du Sancy, and in the last stages runs parallel to the D101 along the ski-tow, the Téléski des Longes.

**Alternative route 2:** Via Station du Sancy to Col de la Cabane du Sancy. In Le Mont-Dore, take the path which starts near the lower station of the funicular railway and leads up towards the Salon des Capucins. Halfway up, you come onto the Sentier des Artistes which cuts across the funicular and, virtually on the level, joins the D101 2 kilometres further on, near a car park. You continue up to the Station du Sancy by following the ski-tow, the Téléski des Longes, along the foot of the ski slopes and parallel to the road. When you come to the large car park, take the track to the left of the cable-ways, leading up to the Pan de la Grange and the Col de la Cabane du Sancy. (See page 47)

**STATION DU SANCY**

⌂

*(ski resort)*
*Cable-car to the Puy de Sancy.*

3.5Km
1:15

From the resort, take the broad pathway which runs clearly to the left of the ski slopes, winding up to the Pan de la Grange and the Col de la Cabane du Sancy (see map ref O).

**Alternative route 3:** PR route to Col de la Croix Saint-Robert. Follow the PR route marked in green which starts in the centre of Le Mont Dore, between the spa and the Hôtel Métropole. The footpath climbs past a waterfall, La Grande Cascade, to the Col de la Croix Saint-Robert.

8Km
3

**Col de la Croix Saint-Robert**
*(see map ref N')*

5.5Km
2

The track climbs gradually up the grassy slopes of the north side of the Roc de Cuzeau (1,737 metres). Take a footpath along the watershed leading downwards at first and then up to the Puy de Crebasse (1,762 metres), and carry on to the Puy de Cacadogne (1,727 metres). Continue to the Pan de la Grange

(1,768 metres); between there and the Col de la Cabane du Sancy, the GR4E comes in from Le Mont-Dore.

## Col de la Cabane du Sancy
*(see map ref O)*
*1,770 m; junction with the GR41 and the GR30 from the Puy de Sancy*
**Detour**, *15 mins*
**summit of the Puy de Sancy,**
*1,885 m*
*From here you can continue on to upper station of cable-car.*

## UPPER CABLE CAR STATION
✗ ⛾ *(summer only)*
*Panoramic map*

2.5Km
0:40

From the Col de la Cabane du Sancy, the GR4, GR30 and GR41 follow the same route, running south-east along the old pathway from Le Mont-Dore to Besse, which follows a contour line. On your left you pass the Puy Ferrand (1,854 metres) and the Puy de la Perdrix (1,824 metres), where the cable-car arrives from Super-Besse. Continue to the Col de Couhay.

## Col de Couhay
*1,685 m*
*point of separation with the GR30*

The GR4 follows the old Sarrevieille quarries path. There are some fine views: from the Roc de Cuzeau across to the Puy de Sancy and into the valley of Mont-Dore; from the Puy de Chandefour, with the Crête de Coq and the Dent de la Rancune.

**Detour**, *2 hrs*
**CHAREIRE**
⌂ ✗
⛾
*1,180 m*

2Km
0:30

**Detour**, see left. Follow the GR30 down to the right, south-west. You can get back onto the GR4 just north of Lac Chauvet by following the GR30 as far as a bridge, the Pont de Clamouze, a distance of 8 km, 2½ hrs.

From the Col de Couhay, the GR4 and the GR41 follow a track running south-east, down past an area of ski slopes and ski lifts. You cross the ski-tow of the Puy de Pailleret and come to the Croix de Seignavoux (1,554 metres). Follow the blue ski slope down to the Lac des Hermines, an artificial lake. It brings you do an old *buron*, or shepherds' hut; you are now in Super-Besse.

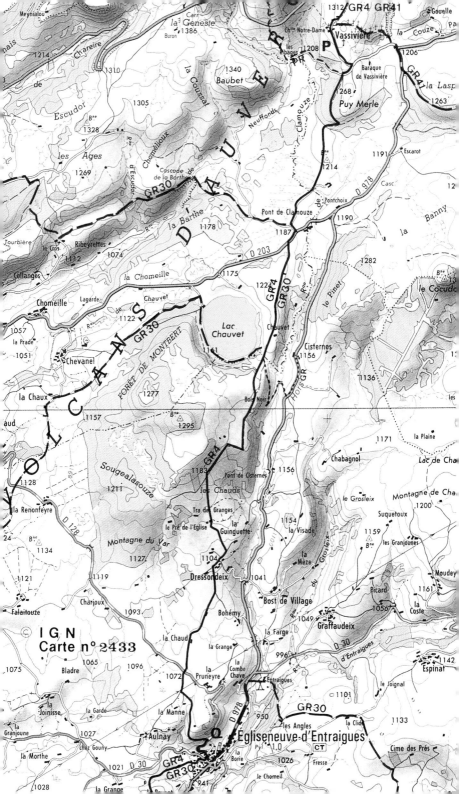

## SUPER-BESSE

⌂ Ⓐ ✕ ☗
🚉 🚌
*1,350 m*
*Ski resort, 8 km from the market town of Besse, purpose built in 1960.*
*A total of 19 ski slopes over an area of 50 km, are open to skiers.*

1.5Km
0:20

Take the path on the same level as the shepherds' hut, following it to the right until you come to the road junction south of the lake. Turn right and follow the D149 for 300 metres, then turn off the road onto a path leading across pasture to Vassivière.

### Notre-Dame de Vassivière

*(see map ref P)*
*1,312 m*
*Point of separation with the GR41, which turns off left towards Lac Pavin, 4 km away.*
*Notre-Dame chapel, which in summer houses a black virgin of Romanesque origin; Notre-Dame de Vassivière, the focal point of a pilgrimage since the 17th century. The virgin is carried up the mountain from the church in Besse, where she is kept during the winter, in a procession called the Festival of the Ascent, and leaves again on the Festival of the Descent on the last Sunday in September.*

3Km
0:45

From the chapel, the GR4 follows a small road, then turns right at the next junction. After 200 metres you come to a road leading straight ahead, west, to a farm, the Ferme des Ribages. Do not take the road, but instead turn left, south, through a plantation of conifers. You cross pasture, climb over a fence near a farm and then bear right across a stream, the Clamouze. Carry on for 600 metres until you come to another path, where the GR30 from Chareire joins the GR4. Turn left and follow the path until you come to the D203, 300 metres west of a bridge, the Pont de Clamouze.

### Pont de Clamouze

*1,190 m*
*Situated near the watershed between the Rivers Dordogne and Allier. It would only take a breach a few metres deep in the virtually flat Col de Vassivère to divert the streams, the Clamouze and the Couze de Pavin, from their natural courses. In winter, the wind and snow caused by the depression, sweep across the plateau making this a dangerous place.*

1.5Km
0:20

The GR4 and the GR30 turn right along the D203 for 100 metres and then take the first turning off to left through a gate and onto a pathway. You pass an old barn and continue southwards until you come to the point of separation with the GR30.

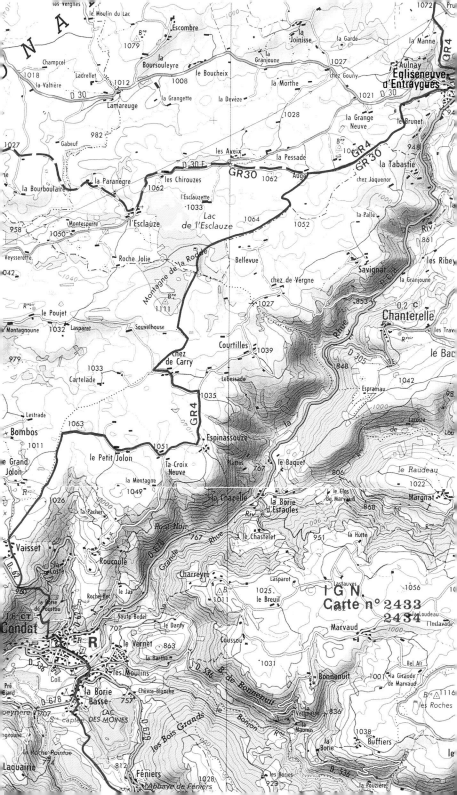

*Point of Separation with*
**the GR30**
*1,278 m*
*Go down to the left, past the barn in the wood, the Bois Noirs, until you come to the D978.*
**Detour**, *40 mins*

6.5Km
1:35

**Lac Chauvet**
*A branch of the GR30 turns off to the right and in 20 mins brings you to the north-west side of the lake.*
**Detour**, *20 mins*
**CISTERNES**
✕ ҳ

**EGLISENEUVE-
D'ENTRAIGUES**
⌂ ⌂ ⛺ ✕ ҳ
🚌
*(see map ref Q)*
*960 m*

3Km
0:45

*Junction with GR30 from d'Espinchal, market town; cheese factory open to public*

Carry on due south, walking alongside some old low walls and close to the wood. After crossing a stream, you follow the barbed wire fencing and then go through a beech grove. You come out onto a broad pathway bordered by fences, which takes you to the hamlet of Dressondeix and, continuing south, across a road (D128). Bear left below a high voltage electricity cable. You skirt round a farm, the Ferme de la Manne, and go down an old path which brings you out further along the D128 leading to Egliseneuve-d'Entraigues.

Take the GR4 from the centre of Egliseneuve in the direction of Saint-Genès Champespe. When you come to the square in front of the cheese factory, turn immediately left along a little street which passes below the market place. A poorly maintained pathway bordered by low stone walls continues on from the street out of the town. It climbs slowly, offering views across Egliseneuve, and then bears left and continues to climb. When you reach the

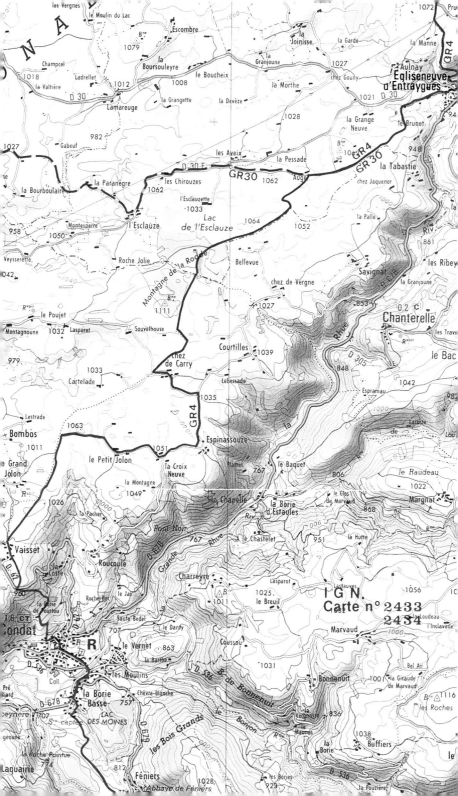

plateau, turn right and carry on south-west, along the pathway bordered by stone walls, to an old farm, the Ferme d'Auger.

### Ferme d'Auger
*1,050 m*
*Just after the farm, the GR30 to Lac de la Crégut, branches off to the right.*

The GR4 climbs to the left, south-west, through enclosed pasture. It is important to follow the GR markings on this section of the route as there are no pathways as such. Follow a fence and bear left towards a marshy area. Climb over the fence, turn right and go slightly uphill until you come across the traces of an old pathway. You pass above a farm, the Ferme de Bellevue, go into a wood and turn due south. Follow the edge of the wood and then bear left, passing below a channelled stream, and come out onto a path leading to the hamlet of Chez de Carry (1,058 metres).

### Chez de Cavvy
*1,058 m*

Turn left onto the path and follow it through the hamlet. When you come to a fork in the road, take the little road off to the right towards Espinassouze, which you bypass by continuing to bear right. Pass through two more hamlets — La Croix Neuve and Le Petit Jolon — and continue straight ahead until you come to a path leading off to the right between two hedges, about 200 metres after the last building on the bend. This old pathway turns sharply and runs southwest, past the village of Le Grand Jolon on your right, to the hamlet of Vaisset. After the first group of houses, pass to the left of the cross and, leaving the road on your right, take the sunken pathway leading off to the left between the hedges and down to the D62. You cross the road to a point slightly to your left, known as the Belvédère de Vaisset, from where a footpath leads down into a copse. Bear right onto a track and then continue right, along a broad avenue of beech trees until you come to a farm, the Ferme de la Borie de Pourtou. You go down through a housing estate and take the first road on the right, which runs along the edge of a vegetable garden. Turn left and then right onto the D679, which will take you into Condat-en-Féniers.

12Km
3

## CONDAT-EN-FÉNIERS

*(see map ref R)*
*706 m*
*Situated in a basin at the*
*confluence of three rivers,*
*La Grande Rhue, Le Bonjon*
*and La Santoire, the village*
*was a prosperous centre of*
*the local cloth trade in the*
*last century.*

**Detour**, *150 m on left*
**Abbey of Féniers**
*12th century Cistercian*
*abbey, rebuilt in the 17th*
*century, with 15th century*
*virgin.*

**Detour**, *30 mins*
**Tranchées de Laquairie**
*Granite platform with faults*
*and fissures of particular*
*geological interest. Carry*
*straight on for 150 metres*
*along a level broad pathway*
*which then turns left onto a*
*footpath climbing fairly*
*steeply to the Tranchées.*

## LUGARDE

5Km
1:15

Go down the main street, across the bridge over the River Rhue and turn immediately right along the river. Before you get to the campsite, go up onto the D678 on a level with a hamlet called La Borie Basse and, almost immediately afterwards, turn off left into a housing estate. At the far side of the estate, leave the grassy pathway on your right and take the old pathway which starts alongside a house, runs between two meadows and then along the edge of a conifer plantation to a pond. Ignore the footpath off to the right and follow the dirt track towards the south-east, which brings you out onto the D16 to Féniers.

Cross the D16 and follow the path opposite, which leads to a small pool. When you come to a junction near a fence turn right along the path bordered by bushes, which will bring you to a grassy clearing. Cross this and follow the footpath down through the undergrowth to the junction of the D16 and the D62, where you cross the Pont des Moines over the River Santoire, in the direction of Lugarde on the D62. Take the second, heavily rutted, pathway on the right, which leads upwards through the woods and brings you out into a clearing.

After the clearing, the GR4 bears left along a woodland path. When you come out of the wood, carry along the path between two meadows. When you come to Chez Pereyre, take the road to the left past some farms, the Fermes des Manicaudies, and continue south to Le Meynial and from there down to Lugarde.

The GR turns left in front of the church of Lugarde. When you come to a wayside cross, turn right and carry on to Lugarde Haute, where you take a track suitable for motor vehicles leading to the bridge across the railway line. The path runs to the right of some pasture and comes back onto the road. Do not cross the railway line at this point, but continue along the road to Regheat, and then along a path suitable for motor vehicles to a farm called La Devèze. Take a path off to the left about 100 metres before the farm and follow it between two low walls, along the edge of a

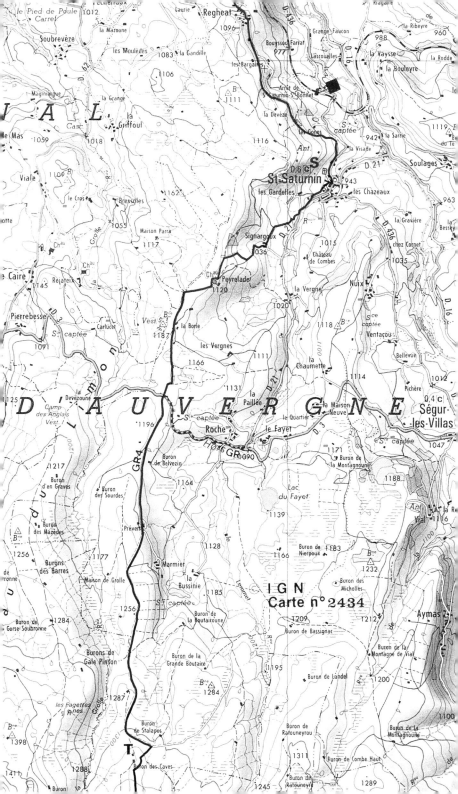

wood and under an electricity cable near a farm, La Ferme des Gones.

**Detour**, *10 mins*
**SAINT-SATURNIN
RAILWAY HALT**

*Turn left along the D436.*

At a wayside cross, the GR4 follows a path to the right leading down to Saint-Saturnin.

**SAINT-SATURNIN**

*(see map ref S)*
*943 m*
*Market town, named after Saturninus, the bishop of Toulouse martyred in 257 AD, is an interesting example of the influences of Aquitaine in the Massif du Cantal during the Middle Ages.*
*Church with 12th century chancel and Romanesque transept extended by Gothic nave.*

4Km
1:10

Turn right at the junction in the village, past the old convent situated in the upper part of town, and continue along a pathway suitable for motor vehicles which will bring you out on the D21. Follow the road for 200 metres; turn off right along a broad pathway which is grassy at first and then becomes stony. Bear left 500 metres further on and follow the path between two low walls and across pasture until it comes to the Ferme de Signargoux. Go past a new barn and take a track which climbs up to Peyralde (where Saint-Nectaire cheese is made). Pass behind the château and follow its access road to the road, where you turn left and continue southwards to the junction with the D3.

**D3**
*1,162 m*
**Detour**, *20 mins*
**PONT DE LA ROCHE**

*Turn left along the D3.*
*Look out on the walk for old burons or shepherds' huts.*

11.5Km
3:30

The GR4 carries on south to a farm, the Ferme de Prévert, then continues in the same direction for 3 kilometres, running along a track suitable for motor vehicles which turns south-east, passing near some shepherds' huts, the Burons de Stalapos. It turns off the main track shortly before reaching them, goes through a kissing gate in the fence on the right and then skirts round to the left of more huts called the Burons des Caves. From there, the GR passes through several kissing gates, following fences towards the south-west and passing near the Buron d'Escourolles. Carry on along the edge of a fence on the left for 3 kilometres until you come to the Puy de Niermont (1,620 metres). From there, the GR runs south-west, down through an area of fallen rocks to an unnamed pass.

**Unnamed pass**
*1,050 m; junction with the GR400*

3Km
0:45

The GR runs south-west along the ridge and down to the Col de Serre.

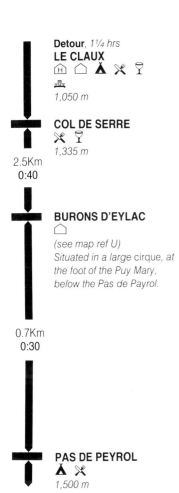

**Detour,** *1 ¼ hrs*
**LE CLAUX**
*1,050 m*

**COL DE SERRE**
*1,335 m*

2.5Km
0:40

**BURONS D'EYLAC**

*(see map ref U)*
*Situated in a large* cirque, *at the foot of the Puy Mary, below the Pas de Payrol.*

0.7Km
0:30

**PAS DE PEYROL**
*1,500 m*

Cross the road, pass behind the café-restaurant and cross a meadow overlooking some woods called the Bois Mary. Follow the ridge down to the road (D680) and continue, to the right of the road, until you come to the Burons d'Eylac.

From the Burons d'Eylac, the GR4 follows the D680 southwest to the tip of a hairpin bend and then takes the old Roman way which passes above the present road.

**Alternative route:** bypassing the Pas de Peyrol and the Puy Mary. Do not cross back over the D680, but turn left onto a footpath which climbs southwards below the Puy Mary and comes out on the watershed at the foot of the Puy.

The GR4 crosses the D680, passes below it along the old Roman way and then climbs up to the Pas de Peyrol.

From the Pas de Peyrol, the GR4 follows the wide stony track leading up to the Puy Mary.

---

**The Pas de Peyrol**
Lying below the summit of the Puy Mary, the pass has always been a thoroughfare, but the road linking it to Aurillac via the valley of the River Jordanne only opened in 1937. The Col is impassable between November and June; patches of snow usually persist until the end of July just above the pass on the northern slopes of the Puy Mary and above the road leading down to Murat. This gives some indication of the harshness of the environment. From the pass, there are panoramic views in both directions. To the north lies the Vallée de Cheylade with its characteristically flat valley bottom, bordered to the west by the Puy de la Tourte and a line of mountains running to La Font-Sainte; to the east by the open spaces of the Plateau du Limon, with the Col d'Eylac in the foreground and the Vallée de l'Impradine overlooked by the Puy de Peyre Arse. To the south lies the pyramidal Roche-Noire and the road, overlooked by La Chapeloune and the Puy Chavaroche as it disappears from view at the Col de Redondet.

**Puy Mary**
*1,783 m*

5Km
1:30

**Col de Cabre**
*1,528 m*

1Km
0:15

**Col de Rombière**
*1,550 m*
**Detour**, *1¼ hrs*
**GARE DU LIORAN**

Go down the ridge to the south-east and follow the watershed along a good mule track and across the Brèche de Rolland.

Carry on along the ridge, ignoring a footpath leading up to the Puy de Peyre Arse (1,806 metres), and follow a path which curves down to the right and brings you to the Col de Cabre.

The GR4 continues on the level, passing below the Puy Bataillouse (1,683 metres) and coming to the Col de Rombière.

**Detour**, see left. At the Col, turn left along the GR400; little further on, go down to the Buron de Meije Costes and carry on to the bottom of the cirque along the right bank of the River Alagnon. Cross a little road and carry on down to the D67 where you turn left to the station.

---

**Col du Pourtou (Portarou)**
Cutting through the watershed linking the Puy Mary to the Puy de Peyre Arse is the Col du Pourtou or du Pourtarou (meaning 'gateway' or 'little gateway'), which has been re-christened with a name curiously reminiscent of the Pyrenees. It consists of two deeply cut, boulder-strewn corridors, leading into each other and provides access between the cirque of the River Impradine and the less clearly defined cirque of the upper reaches of the River Jordanne. A torrent rises at the northern end and tumbles down to the Impradine; while on the gentler, sunny, south-facing slope, is the source of a stream which flows into the Jordanne. Because of their geographical situation, these two corridors provide what has been described as 'a wonderful natural refuge, rather like a botanical garden, where the most characteristic elements of the high peaks of the Massif Central are found together in one place'.

**Col de Cabre**
The Col de Cabre lies between the Puy de Peyre Arse and the Puy Bataillouse. *Cabra* or *cabro* means goat in the dialect of the Auvergne. It is one of the highest passes in the Massif (1,539 metres), but also one of the widest and the most accessible and for this reason lay on one of the main routes across the Cantal region and provided a link between the Valleys of the River Jordanne and the River Santoire for many centuries. In the Middle Ages it was a 'paved way' and 'public royal road'. It was abandoned in the 18th century in favour of the new road which passed via the Col du Lioran, but towards the end of the 19th century was again used by the inhabitants of Dienne to travel to Mandailles on horseback or by cart. Today, it is worn away and barely visible at the top of the pass, but can still be seen along the banks of the Jordanne on the way down to Mandailles, where there are some well-paved and clearly defined sections.

From the Col de Rombière, the GR4 continues along a rocky ridge. After following the ridge, the GR4 comes to a fence. Below and to the right, there is a signpost to the Col de Rombière.

**Detour**, *1 hr*
**Puy Griou**
*1,694 m*

**Detour**, see left. Do not climb over the fence, but follow it to the right and up onto a hillock. As you come down the other side, take a footpath which leads off to the right and along the side of the mountain towards the foot of the Puy. You reach the top by way of a steep path; it is not particularly difficult, although there is a danger of falling stones. On the way down, follow the same track as far as the foot of the Puy and then follow the path which climbs north-east to the 1,618 metre mark and loops down to the left before continuing along the ridge to the Col de Combenègre. Allow 45 mins for the descent to the Col de Combenègre.

The GR4 crosses the fence and leads down to the Col de Combenègre at an altitude (not indicated) of 1,530 metres; at the edge of the forest is the arrival point of the ski-tow from La Font d'Alagnon. Start down a recent ski slope, but bear left immediately back onto the original pathway. You rejoin the slope about half-way along and it brings you quite steeply down to the Col de Font de Cère.

2Km
0:30

**COL DE FONT DE CÈRE**
🏠 ✗ 🍷
*(see map ref V)*
*1,289 m.*
*An important geographical feature, forming the*

**Puy Griou**
Although only 1,694 metres high, the Puy Griou looks imposing because of its steep slopes and isolated position. Like its neighbours Le Griounou and the Puy de l'Usclade, it is composed of fine grained volcanic igneous rock and towers 700 metres above the floor of the valley of the River Cère. Its name appears in texts from as early as the 10th century, which is rare. At that time it was referred to as the Mons Greo: it was thought that the name might come from the low Latin word *grevis* meaning 'hard' or 'difficult' or, alternatively, from the primitive Indo-European root *cara* or *gara*, which always suggests the presence of stone and which has enabled linguists to explain the origins of names such as Pic de Ger or Pic de la Crau.

*watershed between the basins of the River Garonne and the River Loire. The sources of the River Cère, which flows into the Garonne, and the River Alagnon, which is a tributary of the Loire, are only a few hundred metres apart on either side of the pass. Opposite and to the right is the Puy Lioran, otherwise called the Puy de Masseboeuf (1,368 metres); underneath pass the road and rail tunnels, 1,387 m and 1,956 m respectively, which join the two valleys. Before the road tunnel opened in 1847, the road passed via Font-de-Cère and Font d'Alagnon and was not easily negotiable between Le Lioran and Saint-Jacques in winter.*

**1.5Km**
**0:20**

**Detour**, *10 mins*
**VILLAGE VACANCES VAL**
△
*Follow the ski-tow from Font de Cère and go down to the holiday village.*
*Between Le Lioran and Prat-de-Bouc, the route is subject to alteration as a result of land development.*

At the Col de Font de Cère, the footpath turns off sharply from the pass in the direction of the Plomb du Cantal, turning left onto a little road, the upper track. The path then turns immediately left onto the trail leading down through the woods, and comes back out onto the upper track.

**Detour**, *20 mins*
**GARE DU LIORAN**
🚌
*Follow the link path of the GR400 which leads down to the left through Font d'Alagnon.*

The GR follows the tarmac track upwards for 200 metres. On a hairpin bend it continues straight ahead along another track, the Piste Nicolas, and comes to the resort of Super-Lioran.

**SUPER-LIORAN**
🏠 ⛺ ✕ 🍷 ☎ 🚌
*1,238 m*
*One of many tourist development projects financed by Le Cantal département, situated in a*

At Super-Lioran, the GR crosses the meadow from west to east. Ignore the broad grassy track opposite, the Piste du Ramberter, and follow the family track which leads off, slightly to the left, through the woods and then climbs steeply to a platform above the forest where there are some old shepherds' huts. Continue

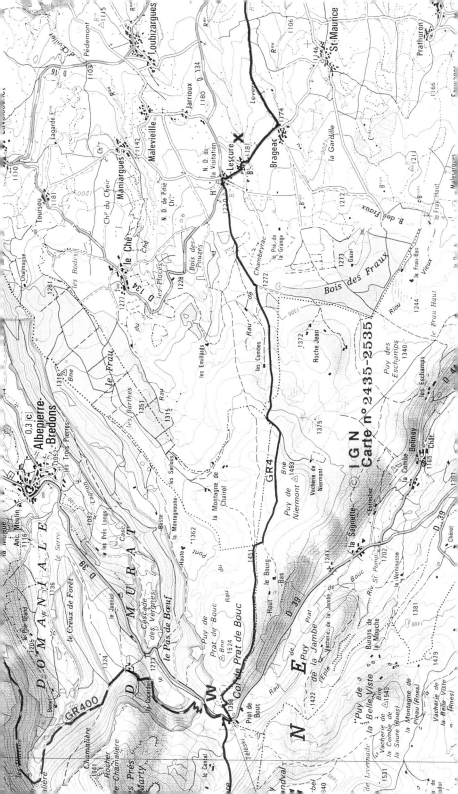

---

**The Plomb**

The Plomb has given its name to the *département* which was formerly the Haute-Auvergne. It was thought that the word *plomb* was a corruption of the word *pomum*, meaning apple or knob, which would describe its rounded summit. As for the word *cantal*, philologers consider it comes from the Celtic root *cant*, meaning shining.

---

4.5Km
2

*meadow, the Prairie des Sagnes, which forms a clearing among pine trees. There are 60 km of ski runs extending across the slopes of the Plomb du Cantal and cross-country ski courses.*

**Plomb du Cantal**
*1,855 m*
*A rounded basalt mound with satellites; the Puy du Rocher to the north, Le Catalou and the Puy Brunet to the south.*

3Km
0:50

*According to legend, the Col is named after a certain Père Récollet, who is said to have died in the snow and been buried there. In autumn, it is a favourite route for woodpigeons migrating to Spain from the Scandinavian countries.*

**COL DE PRAT-DE-BOUC**
⌂ ✕ ⍾
*(see map ref W)*
*The pasture stretching above the Col on the slopes of the Plomb du Cantal, where sheep were brought for summer grazing from Le Quercy, has been converted into extensive ski runs linked to Super-Lioran by cable-car. The Col de Prat-de-Bouc is also a migration route used by more than 10 million birds each year.*

8Km
2

along a narrow track, La Roche, until you come out onto a broad track, the Piste des Alpins, which climbs in wide loops to the Pas des Alpins on the ridge. From here you can get to the upper cable car station where there is a café-restaurant, and from there go on to the Plomb du Cantal.

You come down south-east to the foot of the rocky outcrop which forms the Plomb du Cantal. The GR400 turns off to the right and continues along the watershed to the Puy Brunet. The GR4 carries on down to the left in a south-easterly direction to the Col de la Tombe du Père (1,586 metres). From the Col de la Tombe du Père, bear eastwards down the mountainside to the Col de Prat-de-Bouc.

From the Col de Prat-de-Bouc, the GR4 turns right along the D39 for a few metres, and then turns left and climbs to the Puy de Prat-de-Bouc (1,524 metres). You skirt round to the right (south) of the Puy by taking a stony pathway and then a grassy track running due east along the line of the fences. You pass to the north of the Burons de Bourg and cross the broad hillock of the Puy de Niermont (1,4903 metres). Continue along the marked track which follows the fences and then come down onto a good pathway which carries on towards the east and brings you to Lescure-Haut.

## LESCURE-HAUT

⌂

*(see map ref X)*
*1,200 m*
*The village of Lescure is the focal point of one of the most famous early 18th century pilgrimages of the Upper Auvergne.*

5Km
1:15

## VALUÉJOLS

⌂ ✕ ⌖ ⛴ ▭

*Church constructed in the 14th and 15th centuries with remarkable Romano-Byzantine crucifix, 16th century sculptured stone pulpit, pews and statues.*

## LIOZARGUES

*(see map ref Y).*

The GR4 turns right opposite the church along the road leading down to Lescure-Bas. Carry on towards Brageac, but just outside the hamlet, take a track leading north-east which, further on, loops southwards and comes to Galuse (1,094 metres).

Here you follow the road to the left for 500 metres and just before you come to a large building used for livestock, turn right along an old pathway which follows the line of the fences and brings you out at Valuéjols.

The GR follows the D34 out of Valuéjols in the direction of Paulhac turning almost immediately left down a narrow little street along the side of a large building. The path bears left and comes to a road junction, then turns right along the D16 for 300 metres until it comes to a fork in the road where there is a wayside cross. Take the road off to the left, which brings you to Nouvialou. You cross a little road just below Nouvialou and continue straight ahead along a broad pathway. When you come to a junction, bear right and, passing to the left of a barn, follow a path leading due east, which will bring you out onto the D216 and so into Liozargues.

Turn right along the gravel pathway by the postbox in the centre of the village. You come to a bridge and pass under an electricity cable. Below a farm, you turn left along a dirt track for 600 metres until you come to a broad track. Turn left onto it and follow it until you come to the road (D216), where you turn right and keep on the road for 300 metres. Immediately after crossing a bridge, the Pont des Landes, take a path which climbs to the left, overlooking the River Ander. Just before you come to the high voltage electricity cable, the path leaves the river, then turning right along an old pathway bordered by low walls which leads up through the trees. When you come to a sandy path, turn right along it. You cross the D926, and carry on through the hamlet of Moins. Bear right after the water tower and follow a track suitable for motor vehicles which takes you through a wood, the Bois de Chante-Milan, to a junction.

### Crossroads
*at 907-metre mark*
*Junction with PR route*
*marked in green*

### Roffiac
*Château de Belcastel, largely*
*ruined but with round tower,*
*projecting gallery and*
*section of outer wall; parish*
*church, originally*
*Romanesque chapel of*
*castle; Gothic cross bearing*
*an effigy of Saint-Gal.*

### Le Saillant
*Six-towered château rebuilt*
*in the 18th century and*
*extensively restored during*
*the 19th; la Cascade de*
*Basbories, waterfall formed*
7Km *by two streams which flow*
1:45 *round the basalt outcrop and*
*join at its base.*

**Alternative route:** crossroads at 907 metre mark to Saint-Flour. 2¼ hrs. Follow the path for the PR route marked in green which takes you through Roffiac.

At the junction, the GR bears left. The path follows the edge of the meadows and goes into a wood (the Bois du Saillant), turning northwards and leading down to the railway line which it crosses on a bridge. You come to the D404 at Le Saillant.

Turn right along the D404 and follow it down into the lower part of the hamlet. At the first junction you come to, turn left onto the D40 and then left again at the next junction and follow the road to the village of Andelat (885 metres). Go past the church and turn left along a pathway suitable for motor vehicles which is an extension of the road. When you come to the hamlet of Roueyre, cross the D679 and follow the path opposite for 150 metres before turning right onto a path suitable for motor vehicles overlooking the left bank of the River Ander. Follow the path to Moulin de Massalès.

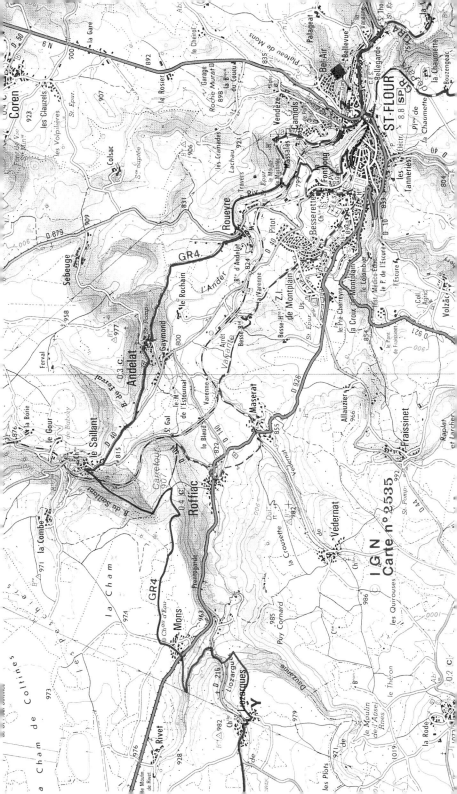

**Moulin de Massalès**
*800 m*

2Km
0:30

**Alternative route:** Moulin de Massalès to Saint-Flour (Ville Basse) direct, 20 mins. Do not cross the river. Carry on along the broad pathway which follows the left bank. After a loop in the pathway, you pass under the railway line near the campsite of the River Ander and the covered market, come into the suburbs. You will come out on a big square, the Place de la Liberté.

The GR crosses the River Ander, follows and then crosses the railway line by way of a little road leading upwards in a broad loop. Go past a new house and turn left onto a path which passes below ' the swimming pool and the gymnasium and comes out into the Rue Blaise-Pascal. Turn left past the post office and then right at the next junction into the Rue du Cardinal-Bernet, a street which winds upwards below the *ville haute* of Saint-Flour. Just after the junction, turn left along a transversal road, the Chemin du Muret, which climbs directly to the Rue de Belloy in the old part of Saint-Flour.

**SAINT-FLOUR**

*Ville Haute*
*880 m*
*Old fortified mediaeval town perched on a basalt outcrop, 14th century gates; 15th century governors' house; 16th century consular house; 15th century cathedral; Musée de la Haute-Auvergne. With many 15th to 17th century houses and mansions, and impressive views from the far end of the Place d'Armes, which overlooks the River Ander and the lower part of the town.*

7Km
0:15

It is possible to reach the lower part of the town from the old town of Saint-Flour.

**SAINT-FLOUR**

*Ville Basse*
*(see map ref Z)*

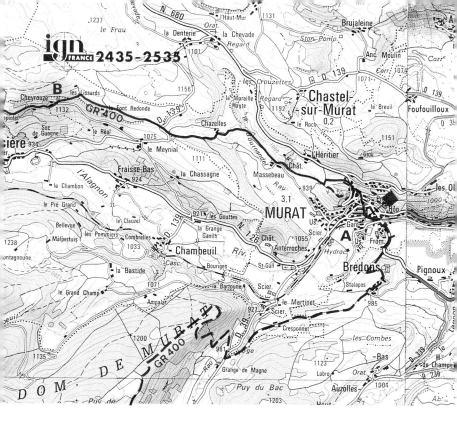

# WALK 3

## MURAT

🏠 🍴 🍷 ⛴ 🚌
👫

*920 m*

*The town's steeply-roofed grey houses cluster in picturesque disorder between the River Alagnon and the Bonnevie rock, a basalt block with famous 'organ pipes' on which stood the old château of the Vicomtes, pulled down in 1633 on the orders of Louis 13th. It had three concentric walls round its central donjon; this had two gardens and a water reservoir in front, with water which was*

From the railway station, go to the town centre and then the church. Go up the Rue de Lavergne, then the Bonnevie path, and turn left.

3.5Km
1:25
*'cold in winter and tepid in summer'. In 1878 a vast statue of Notre-Dame of the Haute-Auvergne was put up on the site.*
*Old town; church, rebuilt in 1494 and restored on several occasions, with statue of Notre-Dame des Oliviers – olive trees – legendarily brought back from the Holy Land.*

**Detour**
**Bonnevie rock**
*Turn left at the first crossroads, up a path without markings.*

At the first crossroads the GR400 turns right and, after crossing the Murat by-pass, runs along the road above the château of Massebeau and then down and across a stream, the Bournandel. From there, it follows a winding path through the meadows and along a hedge to the left to come up again to Chazelles farm. Go down the approach road to this farm onto the road (D139).

**D139**
*1,105 m*
**Detour,** *30 mins*
**LAVEISSIÈRE**
⌂ 𝕏 ✕ 𝖸 ♨
🚌
*935 m*
*Turn left, west, along the D139 for 2 km.*

1.5Km
0:30

The GR400 runs along the D139, northwest, for 100 metres and at the bend turns off down the track opposite, through the gate (close it again behind you). At Font Redonde, where there is a drinking trough continue straight on and, after another 300 metres, before the Buron des Lissards, turn left down to the hamlet of Cheyrouze.

**Cheyrouze**
*(see map ref B)*
*1,132 m*

4Km
1:20

Turn right along the road, which becomes a track. Keep straight on, west, along this track, through the forest; it then curves steeply upwards and makes a definite left turn just below the ridge, reaching the plateau at the huts of Peyre Gary.

**Peyre Gary**
*1,422 m*

3Km
0:50

Walk behind the huts, then left at a right-angle turn. The track goes along the side of the Puy de Seycheuse, through a wood. At a fork 50 metres after the exit from the wood bear right, to the Burons de Vasivière; walk up above them, following a track which curves past a col, altitude 1,495 metres, then bends southwards and reaches two ruined huts overlooking the valley of the Pierre Taillande stream.

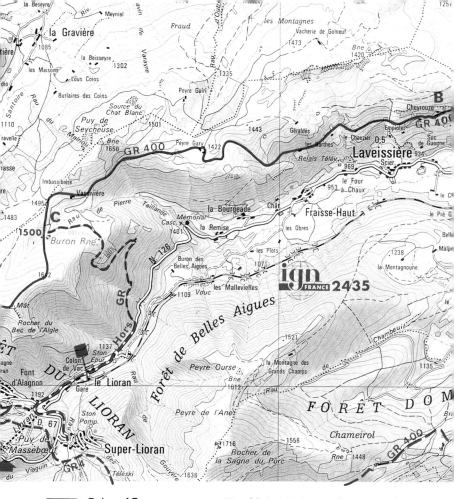

**Ruins of Burons**
(see map ref C)
1,500 m

**Detour,** *1 hr*
**LE LIORAN**
🏠 ✕ 🍷 🚌 🚃
1,150 m
*Turn left, east, on a small track which follows the valley of the Pierre Taillande stream. A series of wide bends brings you down through the wood to the road (N126) leading to Le Lioran.*

3Km
1:20

**Junction**
1,535 m

The GR heads due south, crosses the stream and climbs across the meadow towards two rocky hillocks (1,642 metres). Keep to the right of them, and turn right along a footpath to the Bec de l'Aigle (Eagle's Beak) rock. Continue along the ridge to the west; the footpath passes to the south of the Téton de Vénus (Breast of Venus) and down the side, round the head of the valley. About 200 metres before the east side, of the Col de Rombière, there is a fork.

**Alternative route:** 10 mins, direct to Col de Rombière without descent into Alagnon valley.

From the fork carry straight on, south-west, to the Col de Rombière, where you will meet the marking for the GR4 and GR400 (see page 61).

At the fork, the GR400 takes a sharp turn to the left along a footpath which passes in front of the Buron de la Montagne des Costes. The footpath becomes a track and goes down into the wood through a gate (close it behind you). On the edge of the wood turn right on a track to Font d'Alagnon.

2Km
0:30

**Font d'Alagnon**
*1,195 m*

**Detour** *15 mins*
**LE LIORAN**
Ⓗ ✕ ▽ 🚌 🚃
*1,150 m*
*Take the track opposite, east, then left along the road (D67).*

1Km
0:20

**Detour** *15 mins*
**SUPER-LIORAN**
Ⓗ ✕ ▽ 🚠
*1,240 m*
*Take the track opposite, east, then walk right on the D67, which passes on top of the Lioran tunnels.*

From Font d'Alagnon the GR400 climbs back up an old road to the right, cutting across the bends by following the ski track, to reach the Col de Font de Cère.

**Col de Font de Cère**
*(see map ref V)*
*1,290 m*
*Junction with the GR4*

The GR400 and the GR4 share the same route north as far as the Col below the Puy de Niermont. At the corner of the house, turn right; the track, which is a ski track at the beginning, climbs steeply through the forest to the pastures and the little Col de Combenègre, between the Font de Cère and the Puy Lioran.

**Detour,** *10 mins*
*VAL holiday village*
**SUPER-LIORAN**
⌂

1Km
0:20

*Turn left, by the reservoir, along a track to the gîte.*

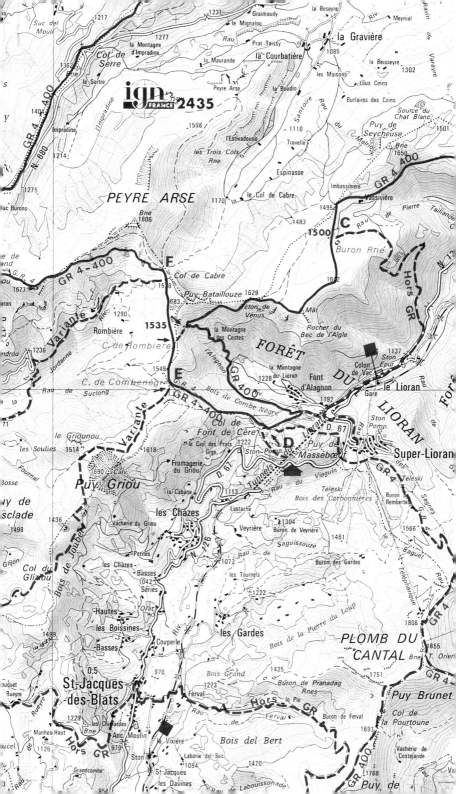

*Detour 3 hrs*
**Plomb du Cantal,**
*1,858 m.*
*By GR4. From the Col de Font de Cère follow the markings south-east to the Plomb du Cantal, as shown on the map. The GR400 here returns to Murat, thus forming a circular walk round the Alagnon valley.*

**Col de Combenègre**
*(see map ref E)*
*1,530 m*
*An important geographical feature, forming the watershed between the Garonne and the Loire basins; the Cère which runs into the Garonne and the Alagnon, which runs into the Loire, rise within a few hundred metres of each other, on the two sides of the Col. Facing the track, at right angles to the Col, there is on the left the Puy Lioran, or Masseboeuf (1,368 metres) with road and rail tunnels (respectively 1,387 metres and 1,956 metres long) beneath, linking the two valleys. Until the tunnel was opened in 1847, the road went via Font-de-Cère and Font d'Alagnon and was very difficult in winter between Le Lioran and Saint-Jacques.*

0.5Km
0:10

**Detour,** *2 hrs 30 mins*
**Col du Pertus**
*1,309 m.*

**Detour**, see left. Take the route south-west marked with a dotted line on the map, skirting Puy Griou, continuing past the Col du Gliziou to the Col du Pertus. (Continue along the GR400 to the Plomb du Cantal and the GR4 from there to Lioran for circular walk of the Cère Valley.)

The GR400 bears right (north) back to the Col de Rombière.

**Col de Rombière**
*1,550 m*
*Junction with direct route*
1Km *north-east to GR400, without*
0:15 *descent into Alagnon valley.*

The GR4 and GR400 continue along a track on the west side of the Puy Bataillouze to the Col de Cabre.

**Col de Cabre**
*(see map ref F)*
*1,528 m*
**Detour** *1 hr 30 mins*
**Liadouze**
*980 m*

4.5Km
2

**Detour**, see left. Walk west and then south-west to Liadouze along the Jordanne valley, following the route marked with a dotted line on the map. You can continue to the Col de Redondet and Pas de Peyrol for a circular walk round the Mandailles valley.

The GR continues north along a footpath across the side of the Peyre Arse and back to the ridge leading to the Puy Mary. There is an awkward stretch at the Brèche de Rolland. At the foot of the Puy Mary it is possible to leave the GR and take an unmarked short cut north, round the Puy, to pick up the GR again on the N680 road to the east of the Pas de Peyrol. The GR goes on up the Puy Mary and back down to the Pas de Peyrol.

**PAS DE PEYROL**
✕
*(see map ref G)*
*1,588 m*
**Detour** *45 mins*
**Col de Redondet,**
*1640 m*

**Detour**, see left. Take the D17 south and then a marked path to the Col de Redondet, following the route indicated by a dotted line on the map. (From there, you can either continue south to Mandailles, Liadouze and the Col de Cabre for a circular walk round the Mandailles valley, or northwest for another circular walk above the Cirque du Falgoux.)

**Detour** *1 hr 30 mins,*
**Col below Suc Gros**
*1,509 m*

**Detour**, see left. Go north on a marked route past the Puy de la Tourte and back to the GR400 at the col below Suc Gros, as shown on the map. You can continue east for a circular walk in the Claux valley, or north for one round the Cirque du Falgoux.

2Km
0:30

At the Pas de Peyrol the GR400 crosses the N680 road. Behind the restaurant, turn right (east), along the Roman way with the road beside and below it. You will cross the N680 again. The short cut round the Puy Mary comes in here from the south. To take it in the

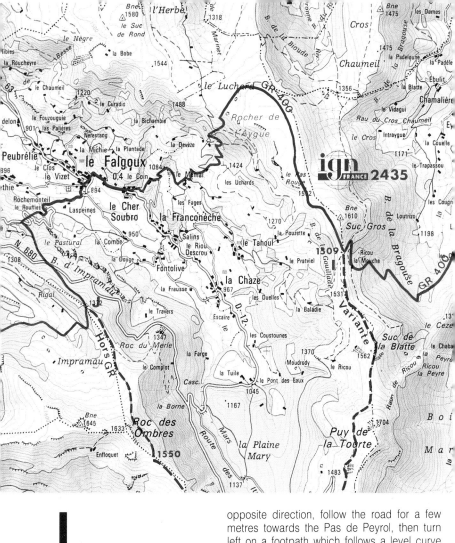

**BURONS D'EYLAC**
🏠 *(summer only)*
*1,423 m*

2.5Km
0:40

opposite direction, follow the road for a few metres towards the Pas de Peyrol, then turn left on a footpath which follows a level curve and rejoins the GRs south of the Puy Mary, before the Brèche de Rolland.

After crossing the road the GRs continue along the Roman way above the road, joining the road again at a hairpin bend and following it to the Burons d'Eylac.

Continue along the N680 road for 600 metres, then turn into the field to the left. The GRs follow the ridge running north-east, roughly parallel to the road, to the Col de Serre.

**COL DE SERRE**

✗

3Km
1:15

*1,335 m*

*Col below the*
**Puy de Niermont**
*(see map ref H)*
*1,520 m.*
*The GR400 and GR4*
*separate here, the GR4*
*continuing straight on, north-*
*east, towards Lugarde and*
*Condat.*

4.5Km
1:20

**LE CLAUX**
**Detour,** *10 mins*
**Village centre**
🏠 ⛺ ▲ ✗ ⛴

🚃

*1,040 m*

3.5Km
1:20

**Étang de Lascourt**
*1,170 m*

4Km
1:20

*Col below*
**Suc Gros**
*1,509 m*
**Detour,** *1 hr 40 mins*
**Pas de Peyrol**
*1,588 m*

3.5Km
1

The path crosses the road (D62) and follows the ridge opposite, north-east, to the foot of the Puy de Niermont.

The GR400 goes down left, west, to the *burons* at La Garde. Turn right here onto a footpath following a contour line, taking you through the woods and across a forest track, to a *buron*. Go past the hut, down through the wood, then across a meadow to reach the television transmitter. Turn left onto the road and follow it to Enchaniers, on the edge of the village of Le Claux.

At the campsite at Enchaniers the GR400 turns left onto the road to Chaumet. Cross the old bridge over the River Petite Rhue and turn right on the D62 for a few metres, to the hamlet of Lapeyre, which has a bread oven. Take the footpath along the edge of the wood to the ridge and then the Étang de Lascourt (pool).

Join the road again and turn left, through Lascourt and then Chaumillous. The GR goes into Bragouse wood and, 500 metres further on, veers to the right and then the left, in clearings. Go round a marshy area, and take a small footpath up to a broad forest track. Turn left along this for a few metres, then turn right off it to the upper edge of Bragouse wood. Go up past a row of trees to reach the ruins of Ricou-la-Mouche, then take a track to the right, and turn left to the ridge at the col at the foot of the Suc Gros.

**Detour**, see left. Walk south past Suc de la Blatte and Puy de la Tourte, following the route marked by the dotted line on the map. You can then continue on one of the two circular walks either to the east around Claux valley, or to the west round the Cirque du Falgoux.

From the col below Suc Gros the GR goes north along the west side of the Suc Gros. Next, bear right through a gap and go down across the open space to the Pas Rouge Col. Continue along the footpath beside a fence a few metres to the right. The path bears left round the Rocher de l'Aygue, then disappears

**Le Luchard**
*1,379 m*

3.5Km
0:50

in the meadow; keep on in the same direction, down towards the shepherd's hut and the low wall furthest to the left. Follow the wall, then another leading on from it, to join a big sheep track to the south of Le Luchard.

Go down the sheep track close by a barn and, 400 metres further on, turn right on a track through Le Ménial to the hamlet of Le Coin. Go down past the back of the houses and on to Le Cher Soubro. From there, take the road, right, to Le Falgoux.

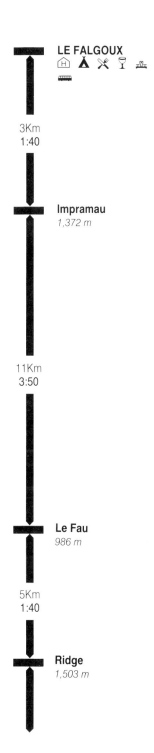

**LE FALGOUX**

3Km
1:40

**Impramau**
*1,372 m*

11Km
3:50

**Le Fau**
*986 m*

5Km
1:40

**Ridge**
*1,503 m*

The GR goes behind the church and to the left of the post office. Turn right, then left. At the bottom of the village turn right onto the footpath across the River Mars to the camp-site. Follow the river-bank to the left, out onto the road, and turn right along it to the edge of Le Rouffier; go up the access road to the farm here, onto the higher road and cross it. Take the forest track opposite, up through Impramau wood and cross the N680 to reach the ridge beside a fence at Impramau.

On reaching the ridge at Impramau, the GR follows the fence on the right, then southwards along the edge of the wood. Climb over a low drystone wall and take, on the right, a muddy track which joins up with a woodland path. Turn left and follow this woodland path for about 2 kilimetres. Take a path on your left which climbs up to Buron du Violental, then turn right towards the Cumine summit.
At the foot of the Cumine, you come to a country path which you follow to the east. It passes at the foot of the Puy Violent (1592m) on the right. Take the path to the right, follow the fence straight down southwards towards a *buron* (shepherd's hut). Climb the fence and continue straight on to the edge of the beech wood. There you will find a path which goes down through the wood to Buron de Cueilles. Leaving the buron on the left follow the fence, turn left and join up with a path on the right hand side. You leave the path and walk through the bracken. Pass behind two houses and go down towards Le Fau.

Follow the road towards La Bastide, walk through the village; at the bridge leave the road and continue straight on towards the Bois Noirs. Take the forest path, pass a gate and continue to the stream, the Aspre. Cross the Aspre and follow the path out of the wood, then go over the Chavaspre mountain passing the buron of the same name. You arrive at the ridge.

Turn right and pass to the west of the Roc D'Hozières. The path follows along the flank of the roche Taillaide. Follow this, continuing south-east, to the Col de Redondet.

### Col de Redondet
*1,640 m*
**Detour** *30 mins*
### Pas de Peyrol
*1,588 m*
*To the east of the Col de Redondet, a marked route joins up with the GR400 at the Pas de Peyrol (see also the map on p. 60). From*

7.5Km
2:10

At the Col de Redondet the GR400 turns right, south-west, on a footpath up to the cairn of Puy Chavaroche. Walk down to your right to a shoulder (see map IGN ref 1620) and then, to the side, return to the ridge and continue to Le Piquet (map IGN ref 1550). Turn to the south-west and follow the north slope of the ridge across a rocky area. The GR next goes down to the two ruined shepherd's huts at Cabrespine. Pass them and bear right to meet

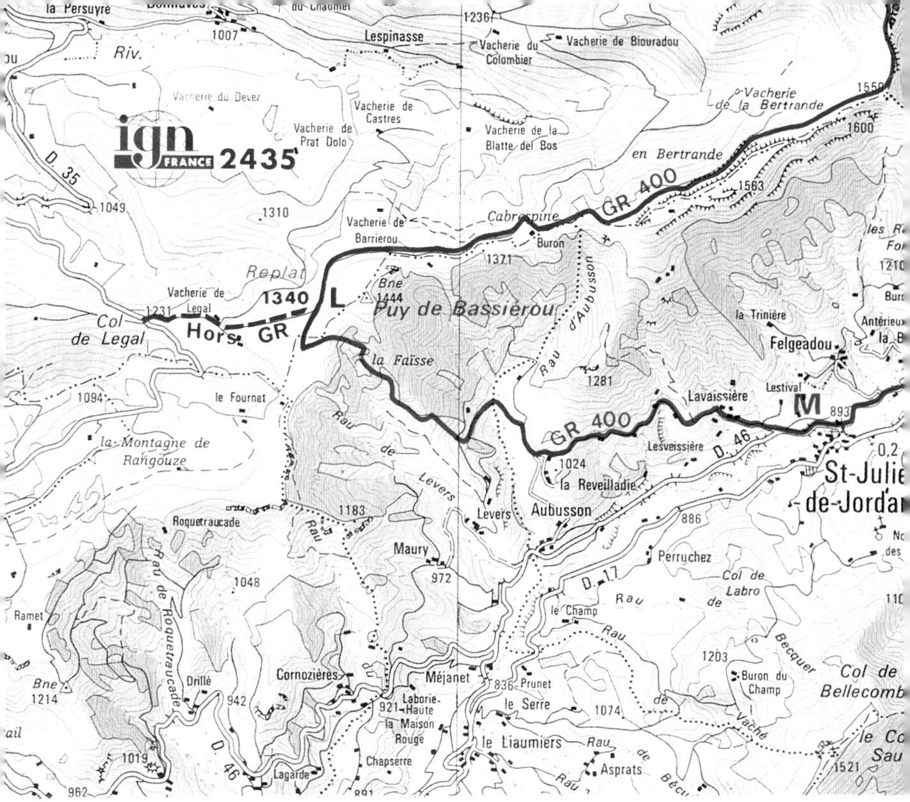


*here, you can continue to make a circular walk round the Cirque du Falgoux, or another circuit in the Mandailles valley, via Liadouze.*

a track coming up from the valley; turn left along it for 2 kilometres to a shoulder beneath Puy de Bassiérou.

*Shoulder below*
**Puy de Bassiérou**
*(see map ref L)*
*1,340 m*
**Detour** *20 mins*
**COL DE LEGAL**
🍴 🍷
*1,231 m*

4Km
1

*Continue westwards on the track past the Legal dairy farm.*

At the shoulder beneath the Puy de Bassiérou the GR leaves the track and turns left across the meadow. It follows a faint track up to the crest, to a wide track below a ruined hut. The track runs down through the beech-wood, below a cliff face then close to a water-tower. Continue along the hillside to a fence, cross it, turn right, cross a hedge and go down across the fields on the access track to a barn. Take the ford across the stream, the Aubusson, and continue along the track close to the Reveilladie farm. Take a wide stone-paved track to Lavaissière and, from there, the road (D46) to Saint-Julien-de-Jordanne.

## SAINT-JULIEN-DE-JORDANNE

⌂ ▲ ✕ 🍷 ⚒
🚌

*(see map ref M)*

1.5Km
0:20

## MANDAILLES

⌂ ▲ ✕ ⚒ 🚌

*924 m*

*At the beginning of the last century Mandailles had eleven water mills. One of these, now smaller than its original size, can still be seen. Turn off the track a few hundred metres before the bridge across the Fournal stream, on to a path coming down from the right to the river (this once led to the village of Rudez). The mill has a steeply sloping stone-tiled roof over its single room, where the milling took place. The horizontal wheel of a now obsolete style, called the* rodet, *was placed directly beneath, on the lower level. A stone near the door is inscribed 'To Combe Jeanne 1717'.*

1.5Km
0:20

## LIADOUZE

⌂

*983 m*

**Detour** *1 km*

## BENECH

⌂ ✕ 🍷

**Detour** *2 hrs 20 mins*

## Col de Cabre

*1,528 m*

*Follow the route, marked on the map with a dotted line, which goes off to the north-east, following the Jordanne valley. At the Col de Cabre it rejoins the GR400. This route makes a circular walk in the Mandailles valley.*

3.5Km
1:25

The GR does not go through the centre of Saint-Julien-de-Jordanne; just before the river bridge, where there is a cross, it takes the road to La Boudie, leaving the road to Le Felgeadou on its left. Where the road bears north towards La Boudie, the GR turns off right along a track to Massoubro. From there it goes down to Mandailles.

In Mandailles the GR crosses the River Jordanne and, 50 metres further on, turns left on a road which leads into a broad track to the hamlet of Liadouze.

The GR turns right, off the *place* in the centre of Liadouze, following the track leading to the old bread oven. The track goes above the waterfall. Cross the field, walking alongside a row of ash-trees; then cross the stream at the ford and climb up between two low walls. At the crossroads turn left; walk past a barn and, 50 metres further on, turn right. This joins up with a footpath coming from Le Tal barn; directly in front of the barn, bear left beside the wood on the track which leads up to the road. Follow the road to the left, to the Col de Pertus.

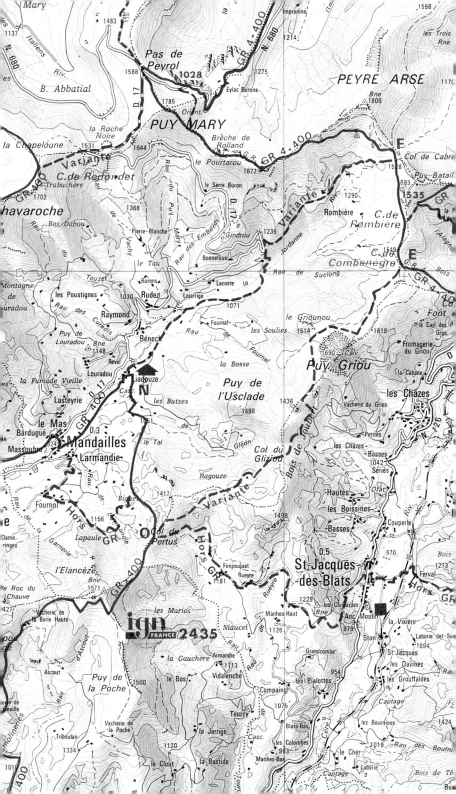

**Col du Pertus**
*(see map ref O)*
*1,309 m*
**Detour** *1¼ hrs*
**SAINT-JACQUES-DES-BLATS**
🏠 ✕ 🍷 ⚏ 🚃
*970 m*
*Follow the road heading east down into the valley.*

**Detour** *2 hrs*
**Col de Combenègre**
*1,530 m*

6.5Km
2

**La Bartassière**
*1,016 m*

4.5Km
1:15

**Detour**, see left. From Col du Pertus, turn north-east on a marked route across Col du Gliziou to the foot of Puy Griou and on to Col de Combenègre, as shown on the map. This can be continued round to make a circular walk in the Cère valley.

The GR400 leaves the road and runs south-west on a footpath through the wood to the ridge. Follow the fence to the right, which leads to the eastern point of the Elancèze. Follow the west point of the same peak to the left, down beside a fence, and, by some rocks, leave it to follow the ridge on the right. Go into the forest, follow a rocky ridge and go down, left, to the huts at La Borie-Haute. Take the track below the Vacherie de Braqueville to a road. Turn left along the road for 300 metres and turn off it before La Bartassière.

Before reaching La Bartassière, the GR turns left on the approach road to the Faillitoux waterfall (this part of the route is private property). Cross the Lasmolineries, the stream at the foot of the waterfall and follow the north edge of the field, which is private property, to the edge of the wood. Find the path which runs along the edge of the wood, leaving a footpath to the right, and, after 1 kilometre, when you are in an open area, turn sharp left, north. Cross a copse of hazel trees and walk up Col de Lagat, where there is a fence. Behind the shepherd's hut there, take a footpath down across the meadow to Lagat farm, and from there follow the road to the right for 1 kilometre, then turn left on the road for Lescure; 300 metres further on, turn off it on a track down to the right, past Confolens and into Thiézac.

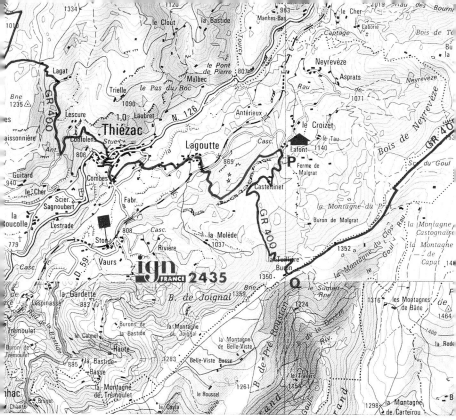

## THIÉZAC

3.5Km
1:30

At Thiézac, take the lane to the left of the church. Walk behind the church, turn right and, 20 metres before the bridge across the Cère, turn left on a track beside the river. Cross the bridge over the river, follow the road east towards Neyrevèze then turn off it at a bend onto a track through the hamlet of La Tour and back onto the road on the edge of Lagoutte. Coming out of this hamlet, go under the railway and, just after the bridge, leave the road on a track up across a rocky area. This crosses two clearings, then meets the foot of a cliff. Do not take the track going down to the left; the GR continues below the cliff, then bears left in the wood.

**Warning:** It is dangerous to continue along the foot of the cliff.

The GR leaves the wood, comes out into a meadow, crosses a stream and reaches Lafont.

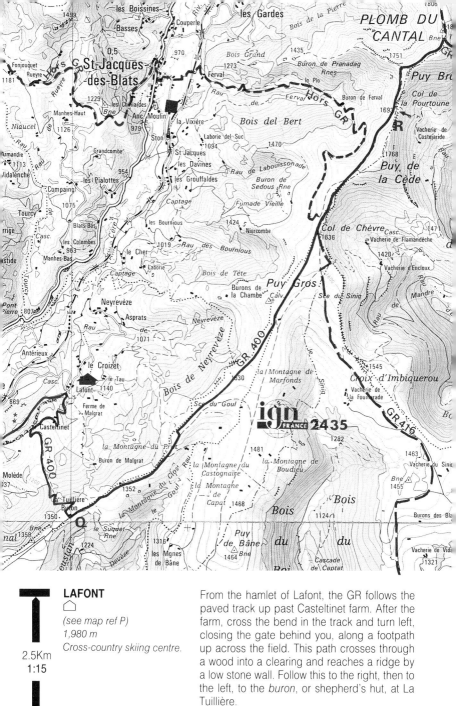

## LAFONT

⌂

*(see map ref P)*
1,980 m
*Cross-country skiing centre.*

**2.5Km**
**1:15**

From the hamlet of Lafont, the GR follows the paved track up past Casteltinet farm. After the farm, cross the bend in the track and turn left, closing the gate behind you, along a footpath up across the field. This path crosses through a wood into a clearing and reaches a ridge by a low stone wall. Follow this to the right, then to the left, to the *buron*, or shepherd's hut, at La Tuillière.

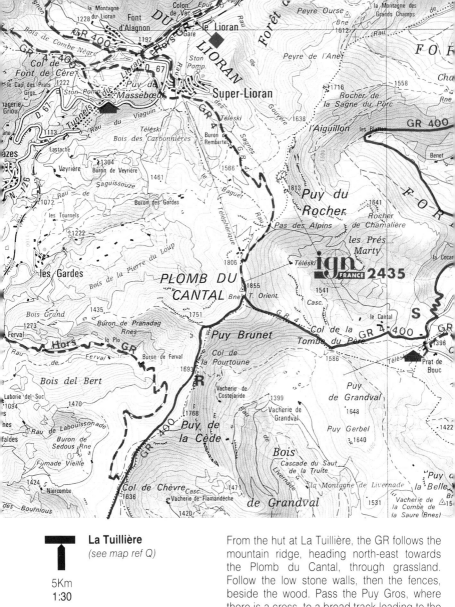

**La Tuillière**
*(see map ref Q)*

5Km
1:30

**Col de Chèvre**
*1,618 m*
**Detour** *1 hr 20 mins*
**SAINT-JACQUES-DES-BLATS**
🏠 🍴 🍷 🚉 🚌
*970 m*

From the hut at La Tuillière, the GR follows the mountain ridge, heading north-east towards the Plomb du Cantal, through grassland. Follow the low stone walls, then the fences, beside the wood. Pass the Puy Gros, where there is a cross, to a broad track leading to the Col de Chèvre.

2.5Km
0:50

*From the col take the footpath left, west, and then north, below the ridge, down to the* buron, *or shepherd's hut, at Ferval, and on to Lo Plo and Ferval in the valley of the little river Ferval.*

Beyond the Col de Chèvre, the GR passes the foot of Puy de la Cède to Col de la Pourtoune.

**Col de la Pourtoune**
*(see map ref R)*
*1,693 m*

Continue northwards along the crest. Do not take the Arpont du Diable, the rocky ridge on the left (see map ref 1751); bear north-east to the foot of the Plomb du Cantal.

**Plomb du Cantal**
*1,858 m*
*Junction with the GR4. Has given its name to the* département *in what was formerly the Haute-Auvergne. There has been much discussion on the origin and meaning of the name. The word Plomb may be a corruption of 'pomum' = 'pomme', apple, which would correspond quite well with the rounded shape of its top. The word 'Cantal' has been linked by philologists with the Celtic root 'cant', shining. It is a rounded basalt hill, with the Puy du Rocher to the north and Le Cantalou and Le Puy Brunet to the south as its satellites.*

3.5Km
0:50

**Detour** *1 hr*
**SUPER-LIORAN**
🏠 ⛺ 🍴 🍷 ⛲ 🚂
*1,240 m*
*Take the GR4 north.*

**Detour** *1 hr 30 mins*
**COL DE FONT DE CÈRE**
*(see p.63)*
🏠
*1,290 m*

**Detour**, see left. Carry on along the GR4 to the Col de Font de Cère to meet the GR400, which can be followed to Murat. From here, you can continue for a circular walk in the Alagnon valley or in the Cère valley (via the Col de Combenègre and, from there, the alternative route to the Col de Pertus, which rejoins the GR400).

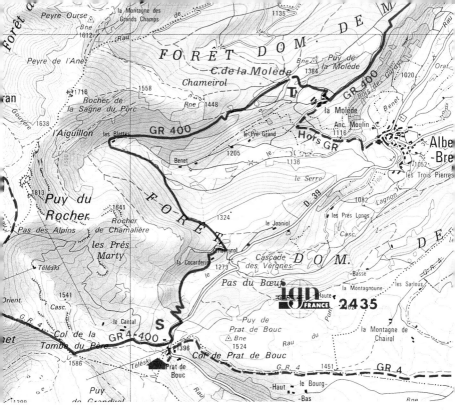

**Prat-de-Bouc**
*(see map ref S)*
**Detour** *10 mins*
**FOYER DE SKI DE FORD
DE SAINT-FLOUR**
⌂
*(Cross-country ski centre)*
*1,396 m*

7.5Km
2

From the Plomb du Cantal to Prat de Bouc, the GR4 and GR400 share the same route. Turn right, south-east, on the footpath down to Col de la Tombe du Père, then bear left, due east, down to Col de Prat-de-Bouc.

The GR4 splits off from the GR400 and heads right, east, to Saint-Flour.

At Prat-de-Bouc, the GR400 heads left, north, along the road for 400 metres, then goes left into the wood on a track which crosses the stream and goes steeply down, still in the wood, to the *buron*, or shepherd's hut, at Raveyrol. Turn left there, along the side of the wood. At the corner of the meadow, turn left on the track into the wood; 250 metres further on, it bears right and joins a forest road. Go left along this to the end, at the Blattes *buron*. Continue heading east on a forest track, which brings you after 1.5 kilometres to the upper Pré Grand hut. From there, take the track north-east to the Col de la Molède. Cross the road and head towards the foot of the Puy de la

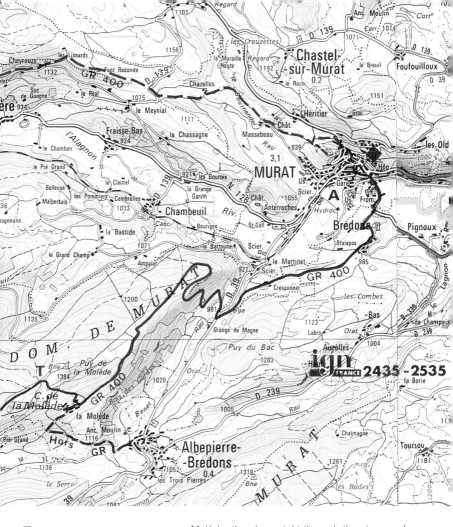

Molède, then bear right through the clumps of broom and take a track going round a meadow to meet a track between ash trees. Go along this track to La Molède.

The GR turns left after the first farm of Molède, then left again at the oratory. It then enters the woods, descends along the crest of the hill, and finally zigzags down to the road (D39) to Murat. If you cross the road you can follow the footpath to the south-east corner of Murat.

**La Molède**
**Detour** *20 mins*
**ALBEPIERRE-BREDONS**
🏠 ⛺ ✕ 🍷 ⚓
1,050 m
*Turn southwest and then east on the road to the village.*

9Km
2:30

**Murat**
*920 m*

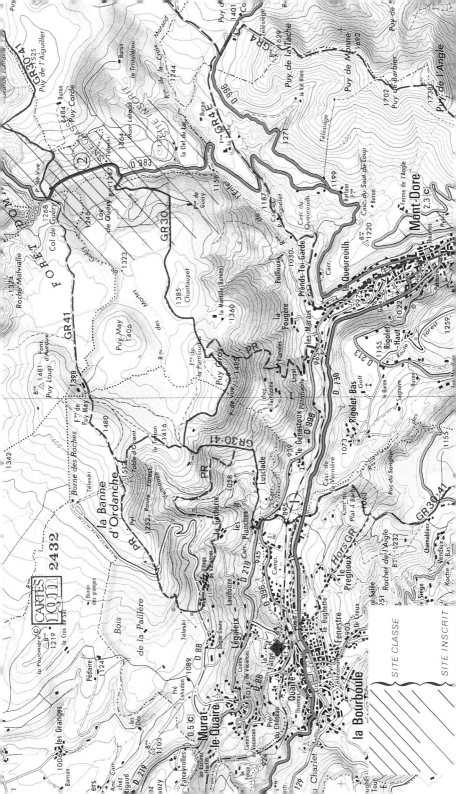

# WALK 4

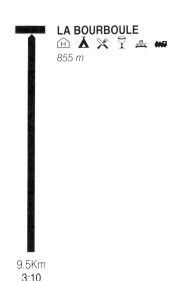

## LA BOURBOULE

*855 m*

**9.5Km**
**3:10**

## LAC DE GUÉRY

(Map ref 2)

*1,247 m*
*At an altitude of 1,247
metres, it is the highest of all
the lakes on the GR30. The
water is contained at the
lower end of the lake by a
small lava flow, reinforced by
a dyke. The Guéry stream,
which rises in the lake, is a*

This section of the route starts 20 minutes out of La Bourboule, on the D130 opposite the path leading to La Vernière (1 on map). Here there are two campsites, Les Cascades and Lers Pardilloux, and a telephone kiosk. Cross the bridge over the River Dordogne and skirt round the Equipment Building. Turn right off the street and cross the railway line by way of the gate. At the hamlet of Les Planches, you come to the D996. Carry straight on for 50 metres and then take the old short-cut which climbs off to the right to Lusclade. Go through the village, continuing in the same direction, and then turn northwards through a beech grove where you begin the climb to the Puy Gros. Just before the pass between Le Tenon and the Puy Gros, the GR30 bears right towards some ruined shepherds' huts while the GR41 carries straight on towards La Banne d'Ordanche. Turn right and follow the footpath which climbs to the Puy Gros. Continue along the footpath leading down eastwards, ignoring a footpath halfway down on the right which is the PR leading down to Le Mont-Dore, and then bear left as far as a fence. Carry on down until you come to a brook and a small marsh, climb over a fence and take the path leading off to the left round the Puy de Chantauzet. Follow the path until it turns southwards, leaving it before it crosses the barbed-wire fencing, and continue to follow the fence eastwards. When you come to the top of the pasture, follow the edge of the pine forest down tô the junction with a gravel forest track. Turn left along it to Lac de Guéry.

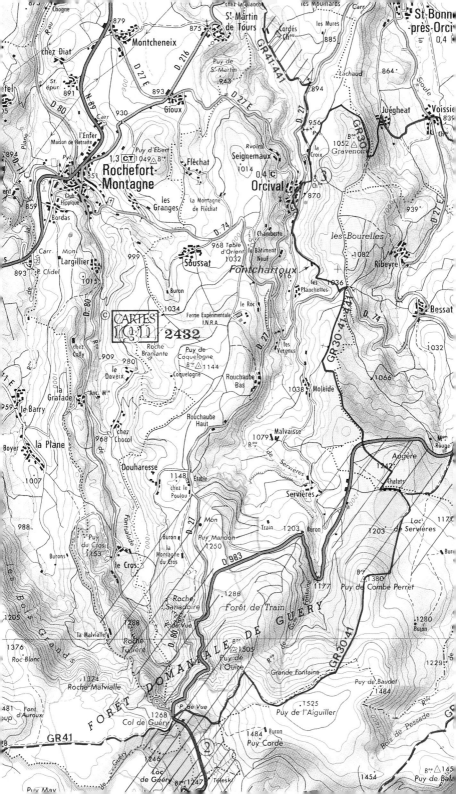

*source of the River Dogne
which joins the River Dore
below Le Mont-Dore to form
the River Dordogne. The
altitude and position of the
lake near Col de Guéry
means that it is often frozen
over for more than 6 months
from November to May.
Between Lac de Guéry and*

6Km
1:50

*Lac Servières, the GR30
crosses the volcanic group
of L'Aiguiller which is also a
centre of volcanic activity.*

### Col de Guéry
*1,268 m*
**Detour,** *250 m off the GR
There is a panoramic view of
the Roche Tuilière, on which
can be seen rainbow
coloured columns of volcanic
rock arranged in bursts of
colour, and the Roche
Sanadoire which is the
remains of an old volcanic
cone.*

At the Lac de Guéry, the GR30 turns left along the D983 to the Col de Guéry.

From the Col de Guéry, the GR30 and the GR41 share the same route. Turn right onto a pathway which climbs up through a spruce forest. As you come out of the forest, follow the fence opposite leading up to the left. Where it divides in two, follow the fence to the left and take the old path which climbs up along the edge of the plateau, bringing you to the Col de l'Ouire (1,436 metres). Bear right and climb over a fence.

**NB:** the GR30 passes through private property until it reaches the Lac de Servières. Follow the GR markings carefully and keep to the ridge.

The GR30 climbs along the edge of the plateau and then the upper edge of the forest until it reaches the Puy de Combe-Perret. Here you turn right and continue along the edge of the wood to the Lac de Servières. Follow the lake round to the right as far as the chalets.

### Roche Sanadoire
A castle used to stand on the summit of the cone which, until the 15th century, served as a refuge for the bands of mercenary soldiers who terrorised the region during the Hundred Years' War.
It might seem surprising that the Roche Sanadoire was able to support a fortress, even one of modest dimensions. It seems reasonable to suppose that its surface area and summit were substantially reduced by an earthquake, possibly the one that shook the region so violently in 1477, seriously damaging the Romanesque church of Orcival. This tremor was followed by an even stronger one in 1490.

### Lac de Servières
*1,203 m*

### Detour
### PESSADE

*The GR441 leads eastwards
to Pessade.*

5Km
1:20

### ORCIVAL
*870 m*
*The church was built for a
pilgrimage in honour of the
Virgin, which still goes on
today. Made of volcanic rock
from the Monts Dore, it has a
somewhat austere
appearance. Orcival is a fine
example of the Auvergne
taste for restraint, balance
and moderation. The*

The GR30 and the GR441 share the same route.

After the last chalet on the Lac de Servières, turn right along a pathway through the wood, and 200 metres further on turn sharp left. You cross the D983 after 500 metres and take a farm track opposite leading through the wood. When you come to the other side, turn left for 100 metres and then turn right onto a gravel track which brings you onto the D74. Turn left along it for 100 metres and then turn sharp right onto a path which takes you past a farm, the Ferme de la Fontchartoux, where there is a *gîte*, and down onto a road which, to the right, leads to Orcival.

### Lac de Servières
The lake was previously much bigger shown by the existence of an old shore terrace 50 cm above its present level. Its shores slope gently on all sides. This attractive stretch of water or *maar* is probably the result of a crater being pierced by a violent explosion. It would seem that the lake occupies the site of the last crater of a huge volcano with three mouths, the two other centres being the Puy de Combe-Perret in the north and the Puy de Servières in the south. All these structures belong to the period of volcanic activity of the Monts Dore which dates back to the Tertiary Period and is therefore much earlier than that of the Chaîne des Puys. Surrounding the lake is a large forest of spruce and scotch pines. Neither species are native to the region, but are extensively used in reafforestation.

*columns of the basilica are beautifully decorated with foliage and animals. In the nave, a carving illustrates the torture of the miser. The face of the Virgin of Orcival is not symmetrical: it is both the face of an Auvergne peasant woman and a lady of high birth.*

**5Km**
**1:30**

*Separation of*
**the GR441 and the GR30**
**Detour (GR441)** *20 mins*
**Château de Cordès**
*The Interior is decorated with stuccowork. The 15th century chapel contains a statue of the Maréchal d'Allègre who died at Ravenne in 1512. The 13th to 15th century manor and its formal gardens provided the setting for Paul Bourget's novel,* Démon de Midi *(Demon of Midday).*

**Neuville**
*965 m*

**Junction with the GR33**

**2.5Km**
**0:45**

**Recoleine**
*933 m*

**3Km**
**0:45**

When you have passed the church in Orcival, bear right in the direction of Clermont and continue up to the D27. Cross the road and take the footpath opposite leading up to a chapel. This section of the GR30 is shared by a PR route marked in blue. Turn left and carry on to the hamlet of La Croix.

In the hamlet of La Croix, the GR30 follows a path leading off to the right, passing near an electricity pylon. Bear right 300 metres further on and skirt round the Puy de Gravenoire. When you come to a pathway 1 kilometre further on, turn left along it to Juégheat. As you come into the hamlet bear right after the first house and follow the little road which leads downwards, skirting round the grounds of the château. You cross the D27E near the public washing place in Voissieux, and go through the village to the right. Take the pathway bordered by tall alders which runs along the banks of the Sioule stream. After crossing the stream, bear left along a grassy track leading upwards. Carry straight on to Neuville.

From Neuville, you continue downwards for 100 metres and then bear left. When you come to a wide junction, take the path leading down to the right towards a small valley. You cross the Gorce stream on two large, flat stones. Continue upwards, ignoring two pathways off to the right, until you come to a little road where the GR30 joins the GR33.

The GR33 and the GR30 share the same route as far as La Cassière, and both follow a gravel track eastwards as far as Recoleine.

Cross the N89 at an angle and take the narrow street opposite near the drinking trough. You come to the main street of the village where you turn right. At the corner where there is a drinking trough the GR follows a stony track upwards. You come to a road which you leave immediately at a bend, and continue upwards in the same direction to a broad pathway running due east, bordered by dry stone walls. Near the Puy de Pourcharet on the left and the Puy de Montgy on the right, the footpath

## The Chaîne des Puys

A chain of independent volcanic mouths where the lava flows follow the present system of waterways. The volcanoes stand on a narrow plateau overlooking the River Limagne to the east, and running north-south along the middle course of the River Sioule for about 30 km to the west. There are more than 60 volcanic structures with an average height of between 1,000 and 1,200m. The Puy de Dôme stands out above the rest with an altitude of 1,464m. It also differs in that its dome consists of domite which is quite unusual in this area. The volcanic cones, which have remained untouched by erosion, indicate very recent volcanic activity. Tests show that they go back scarcely more than a few thousand years. The greater part of the Chaîne des Puys has been extensively reafforested since the 19th century.

crosses the heathland, following the marks on the ground. You follow the edge of a coniferous plantation on the slopes of the Puy de Montjugeat, and then come to the centre of a depression surrounded by volcanoes where there is a signpost.

### Signpost

(See map ref 5)
*1,044 m*
*Junction with the GR4 and the GR441*
**Detour (GR4)** *1 hr*
**LASCHAMP**

2Km
0:30

At the signpost the GRs turn right, passing along the foot of the Puy de Lassolas and the Puy de la Vache.

### Puy de la Vache

**Detour** *30 mins*
**CHÂTEAU DE MONTLOSIER**

## Puy de Lassolas and Puy de la Vache

These volcanoes with their jagged craters are the two jewels of the Chaîne des Dômes. It is well worth spending a hour or so in these craters: the stunted junipers, heathers and pines create a striking landscape.

The lava flows from the Puy de la Vache and the Puy de Lassolas forced their way southwards, filling a valley and serving as a dam for all the tributary valleys whose waters were stopped by the volcanic wall. In this way, about twelve lakes were formed. Most of them were fairly shallow and gradually dried up. Only the Lac de la Cassière and the Lac d'Aydat remain as testimony to the strength of the dykes constructed 7000 years ago.

**3Km**
**1**

*Visitor information about the Parc Naturel Régional des Volcans (Regional Volcanic Nature Reserve of the Auvergne).*

Turn right at the junction in front of the Puy de la Vache. You carry straight on along the path leading through the trees and come out onto the D5 in a large grassy clearing. At this point (IGN ref 978) the GR4 and the GR441 leave the GR30 and the GR33 and turn off to the right towards the Col de la Ventouse (6 on map). Cross the D5 and take the wide forest track opposite which runs through the trees and brings you out onto grassy moorland dotted with junipers and birches. The GR turns left onto a path which runs alongside the N89, and then crosses it at an intersection at the place known as La Cassière.

### LA CASSIÈRE

⌂ ✕ ♆

*950 m*

*From the footpath overlooking the Lac de la Cassière you can see that the lake lies in a depression which has been blocked off at its lower end by a rocky rim formed by the volcanic lava flows from the Puy de la Vache and the Puy Lassolas. The lake is fed entirely by the water circulating beneath the lava flows.*

**4Km**
**1:10**

After crossing the N89, follow the road to Aydat for 100 metres and then bear left along a pathway leading upwards along the edge of some conifers and passing twice beneath a high-voltage electricity cable (see 8 on map). Th GR33 goes off to the left towards Saint-Saturnin. The GR30 turns right along a broad pathway leading southwards. At the end of the path, turn right and continue as far as a wayside cross where you turn left and follow an electricity cable. After the first house you come to, turn right in front of an electricity pylon, follow the edge of the meadow and then turn left onto a footpath which runs through a wood and brings you out onto a road. You turn left along the road and come to the D213 just to the west of Rouillat-Bas.

### ROUILLAT-BAS

⌂ ⚑ ✕ ⚒

*827 m*

*To the west of Rouillat-Bas, the GR30 runs across the rugged surface (cheire) of the lava flow of the Puy de la Vache to the village of Le Lot.*

**2.5Km**
**0:40**

Just outside Rouillat-Bas, the GR30 crosses the D213 and carries straight on to the hamlet of Le Lot (9 on map). Turn right at a 'no through road' sign (*voie sans issue*), cross the overflow of the Lac d'Aydat and follow the path leading off to the right along the hillside. When you come to the shore of the lake, the path climbs to Poudure.

---

### Lac d'Aydat

Several thousand yeas ago, the River Veyre flowed where the Lac d'Aydat is today. Its valley was obstructed by the lava flows of the Puy de la Vache and the Puy de Lassolas as they made their way down to Ponteix. As it leaves the lake, the Veyre disappears beneath the lava flow, reappearing near Saint-Saturnin.

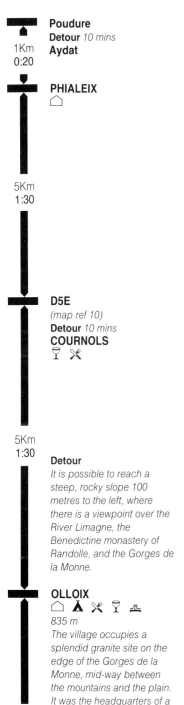

**Poudure**
*Detour* 10 mins
**Aydat**

1Km
0:20

**PHIALEIX**

5Km
1:30

**D5E**
*(map ref 10)*
*Detour* 10 mins
**COURNOLS**

5Km
1:30

**Detour**
*It is possible to reach a steep, rocky slope 100 metres to the left, where there is a viewpoint over the River Limagne, the Benedictine monastery of Randolle, and the Gorges de la Monne.*

**OLLOIX**
*835 m*
*The village occupies a splendid granite site on the edge of the Gorges de la Monne, mid-way between the mountains and the plain. It was the headquarters of a*

In Poudure, the GR30 takes the first road on the left leading up through a housing estate. You then turn left onto the path leading to Phialeix.

The GR30 passes to the left of Phialeix and continues to the top of the hill and over a pass. Carry straight on, turning left and then right 50 metres before you come to a road, the D145, which you cross and carry straight on along a sunken pathway leading down the hamlet of Le Mas. You pass to the right of the hamlet and come out at the top of an area of commonland where there is a cross. Take the broad gravel track at the bottom end and then bear right along a footpath. Further on you turn right along a broad pathway southwards. When you come to a fork, turn right and then left. When you reach the D5E, turn left along it for about 100 metres.

The GR turns right along a broad gravel track which leads southeast and then curves back towards Cournols in a broad loop. The dolmen of Cournols stands 50 metres off to the left. You come out onto the D145E where you turn right. Turn right again after 100 metres, along a lane and a little further on take the path leading off to the right towards a pinewood. Follow the edge of the pinewood and then continue southwards, keeping to the left of a hedge.

The GR follows a footpath which winds down into the Gorges de la Monne. You cross the river by way of an old stone bridge and pass through the ruins of the hamlet of Ribeyrolles. When you come to the plateau, turn right at the junction and then turn right again 500 metres further on. The path runs along the edge of the cemetery and comes to the village of Olloix.

**8.5Km**
**2:30**

*powerful commandery of soldier-monks. Little is known of its origins but Romanesque elements of the church suggest that the commandery was already in existence in the 12th century. It was probably founded by the order of the Knights Hospitallers. Remains of the fortifications near the 12th and 15th century church, which contains tomb of Odon de Montaigu, (Saint Gouérou, 'the warrior') prior of Auvergne for order of Knights Hospitallers.*

**Detour**
**Puy de Mazeyres**
*panoramic map*

### SAINT NECTAIRE

*710 m*

**Detour** *20 mins*
### SAINT-NECTAIRE-LE-BAS

*Here you will find a dolmen, a park and thermal springs. Take the street on the left.*

**7Km**
**1:45**

*The church of Saint-Nectaire-le-Haut is one of the masterpieces of Romansque art in the Auvergne. It contains relics of Nectaire, one of the first apostles of the Auvergne. The only church in the Auvergne possessing a narthex which has not been restored in any way; remarkable series of illustrated columns arranged around altar; admirable reliquary, bust of Saint Baudime (a masterpiece of*

In Olloix, the GR crosses the D74 and carries straight on up the pathway opposite. When you come to a junction, bear left round the Puy d'Olloix southwards until you come to a broad dirt track. Turn sharp left and go down into a small valley where, 800 metres further on, you turn right onto the pathway leading up onto the Plateau de Chabarot. Turn left and then left again at the junction of three pathways and carry on down to the hamlet of Lenteuge. Follow the D150 for 50 metres southeast and then turn onto a pathway leading down to the right. After the bridge at the bottom of a small valley, turn right onto a pathway which crosses the D150 just outside Sauvagnat and then leads up onto the Plateau de Sailles. You cross the D74E and carry straight on down the pathway opposite which brings you out onto the D150 opposite a transformer.

The GR30 follows a pathway off to the right which leads down between steep banks to Saint-Nectaire.

The GR30 continues down to the square in front of the town hall and church in Saint-Nectaire-le-Haut.

Cross the road and take the street opposite, the Rue des Grottes de Châteauneuf. You turn left and then right, passing a *gîte*, Le Clos du Vallon, and come to the lower part of the town. This section of the route is shared with a PR route marked in yellow. After crossing the D996 and then a bridge, follow the road opposite for 200 metres before bearing right along a pathway. When you come to a fork, take the path to the left which brings you to the D150. Turn right along the D150 and then left after 100 metres you turn right at the next junction and come out onto the road just outside Sapchat. Turn right along it for 100 metres and then left onto a pathway. After bearing right between two low walls, follow the

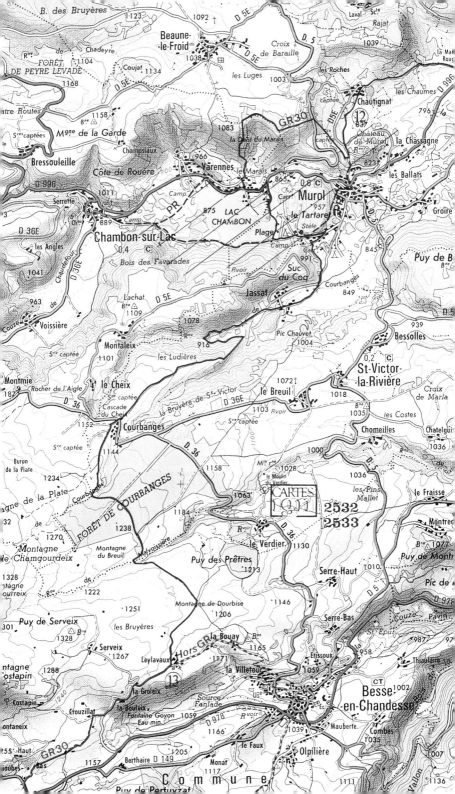

*Limoges metalwork); enamelled book bindings.*

pathway through a wood to the D996. Here you turn left, and then right after 100 metres, onto the broad pathway leading up to Chautignat. Just outside the hamlet, take the path leading down to the left and across a stream. Cross the D5E and carry straight on until you come to the car park on the embankment near the Château de Murol.

## Château de Murol
*890 m*

*The château occupies a strategic position at the crossroads of important communication routes. According to historians, the château was already in existence in the 6th century. In the shape of an irregular twelve-sided polygon, this impressive structure is built of dark, reddish lava which emphasises its romantic appearance.*

**Detour** *10 mins*
**MUROL**

5Km
1:30

After the car park of the Château de Murol, the GR follows the path which leads off to the right through the pine trees and up to the D5. Cross the road and carry straight on along the footpath opposite which climbs the slope and brings you out onto the ridge of a cirque, La Dent du Marais. Keeping well away from the edge of the cliff, follow the ridge to the right. At the far end, you go down until you come to a broad pathway. Follow this to the right for 150 metres and then turn right and then to the left of the transformer. Flights of steps bring you to Lac Chambon where you follow the road to the left for 300 metres and then turn right onto the road leading to the beach. Cross the footbridge and then the beach to reach the southern edge of Lac Chambon.

## LAC CHAMBON
*875 m*

The GR30 turns left along the access road to the campsite. At the junction at the foot of the Puy de Tartaret, carry on along the road for 300 metres and then turn sharp right onto the first pathway you come to leading to some detached houses. When you come to the forest, turn left along the path which runs along the edge of it and, 500 metres further on, cuts

---

### The Puy de Tartaret

Formed across the U-shaped glacial valley of La Couze de Chaudefour. It created a barrage lake 2km in length of which the barrage was later reinforced by a landslide from La Dent du Marais. Tartart has a flattened, elliptical crater, doubled on its northern side by a crater breached to the west. The longest lava flow stretched from the eastern foot of the Puy down the valley to Neschers, 22km away. It is the longest basalt lava flow with a rugged, fragmented surface (*ceire*) in the Auvergne. The upper part of the flow from Murol to Sapchat (1km by 2km) is covered with about 40 little cones of between 5 and 30m in height. They are a kind of miniature volcano probably formed by secondary eruptions linked to the extensive vaporisation of water which took place as the lava flow spread across the marshy surface.

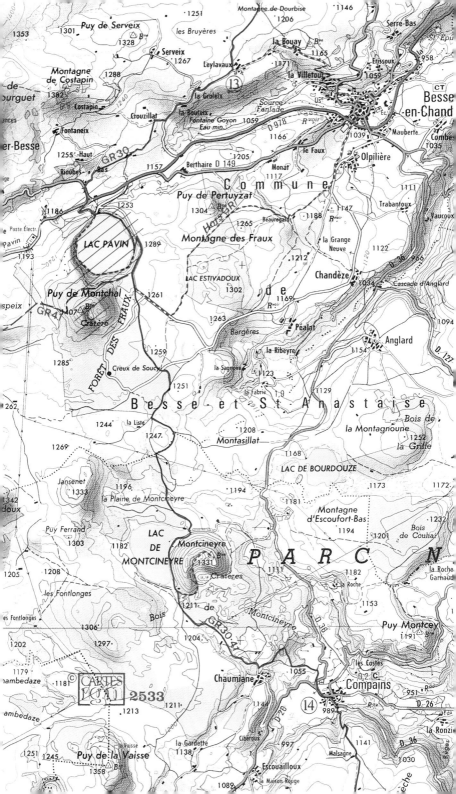

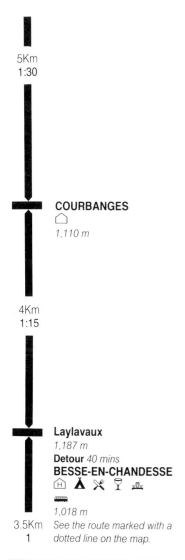

5Km
1:30

**COURBANGES**
*1,110 m*

4Km
1:15

**Laylavaux**
*1,187 m*
**Detour** *40 mins*
**BESSE-EN-CHANDESSE**

*1,018 m*

3.5Km   *See the route marked with a*
1       *dotted line on the map.*

across a road. Cross the road and carry straight on. You cross a bridge and then turn right onto a dirt track which brings you to the village of Jassat. After the last house, follow the path along the right bank of a stream, the Courbanges. You cross two bridges and, after the second, follow the path round a hairpin bend to the left. Continue up along the edge of a wood and, after a bend to the right, climb steeply into the forest. As you come out of the forest, you follow the edge of some terraces and then a broad dirt track which bring you to Courbanges.

At Courbanges, the GR crosses the D36 and follows a broad dirt track opposite which leads upwards and bears slightly left. Follow the track until you come to a stream, the Courbanges, which you cross by way of a bridge, and then carry on through a 19th century forest, the Forêt de Courbanges. The GR turns left along a narrow footpath which crosses an access road, the Grande Allée, and carries on to the southern boundary of the forest. Carry straight on along a fence and across a stream, the Malvoissière. Follow the fence up the opposite side of the small valley. When you come to some barbed-wire fences, carry on between them to the hamlet of Leylavaux.

At Leylavaux, the GR turns right along the road as far as the access road to the Domaine de Crouzillat. Opposite the farm, you climb over a fence and carry on across pasture to another farm, the Ferme de Sagnes. Leaving the farm buildings on your left, carry straight on along the access road to the farm. When you come to Rioubes-Bas, take the road to the left, cross a bridge and continue to the left along the

**Lac Pavin**
Lac Pavin is the most impressive of the lakes of the Auvergne. Due to humus-rich soils fossilised beneath the volcanic deposits, it has been possible to date its formation as having taken place 3500 years ago. The shores of the lake are very steep, continuing to slope steeply underwater beyond a narrow ledge (*beisse*) just below the surface. The floor of the lake is level. Lac Pavin is fed by many springs, several of which probably rise below the lake. The water in the depths of the lake is always very cold. Even at the height of summer, it is between 4–5°C at a depth of 20m. The lake is well-stocked with trout and char.

**LAC PAVIN**
🍴 🍷
*1,200 m*

5Km
2:15

**Detour** *30 mins*
**Puy de Montcineyre**
*Take the footpath leading up*
*to the left through the trees.*

D149. You pass to the right of the petrol station and take the road opposite leading to Lac Pavin.

The GR passes the restaurant and follows the path which runs eastwards, skirting round Lac Pavin to the left. You turn sharp left onto a footpath which climbs the rim of the crater and comes out onto a little road. Turn right along it for 300 metres to its highest point where the GR41 joins the GR30 and shares the same route as far as Brion. Continue along the road and then leave it to follow the edge of the forest. You cross two new access roads leading to the Grotte du Creux de Soucy (Cave of the Creux de Soucy). After an enclosure at the southern edge of the forest, climb up to the left, through pasture, to the top of a hill from where there is a view over the Lac de Bourdouze. Follow the fence leading down to the right and then continue along a pathway until you come to an artificial pool. Take the gravel track opposite which leads up along the edge of plantations and brings you out at the Lac de Montcineyre. Follow the shore of the lake, round the foot of the Puy de Montcineyre, until you come to its southern edge.

The GR30 and GR41 join a pathway which climbs straight ahead, crosses a meadow and bears left through a gate. Leaving a farm on your right, you go down to the hamlet of Chaumiane.

**Lac de Montcineyre**
The lake follows the line of the Puy de Montcineyre to the east. The lava flows from the Puy reached as far as Compains, 7km away, where they spread along the bottom of the U-shaped glacial valley of the Couze de Valbeleix.
The formation of the volcanic cone, blocking a wide depression, seems to have created the Lac de Montcineyre. It is fed by streams which rise under the lava flow on its southern edge. The water leaves the lake by way of deep underground fissures which come to the surface about 2km away. The lake contains excellent perch, trout, pike, and bleak. There is a very beautiful beech copse on the Puy, with interesting lichens. A feature of Montcineyre are the skeletal lava pellets that it has showered over the surrounding area of nearly 30km$^2$. Amongst the volcanoes of the Chaîne des Puys, only the Puy de la Vache and the Puy de Lassolas have such a wide range of activity. The lava flow reaches a depth of 10m at the eastern foot of the volcano, where it is mined.

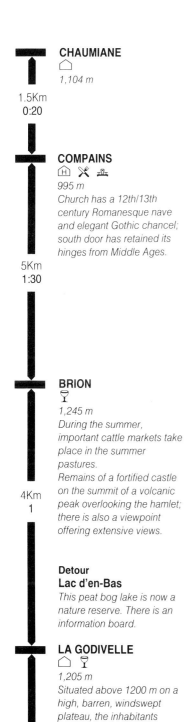

**CHAUMIANE**
⌂
*1,104 m*

1.5Km
0:20

**COMPAINS**
Ⓗ ✕ ⚒
*995 m*
*Church has a 12th/13th*
*century Romanesque nave*
*and elegant Gothic chancel;*
*south door has retained its*
*hinges from Middle Ages.*

5Km
1:30

**BRION**
🍷
*1,245 m*
*During the summer,*
*important cattle markets take*
*place in the summer*
*pastures.*
*Remains of a fortified castle*
*on the summit of a volcanic*
*peak overlooking the hamlet;*
*there is also a viewpoint*
*offering extensive views.*

4Km
1

**Detour**
**Lac d'en-Bas**
*This peat bog lake is now a*
*nature reserve. There is an*
*information board.*

**LA GODIVELLE**
⌂ 🍷
*1,205 m*
*Situated above 1200 m on a*
*high, barren, windswept*
*plateau, the inhabitants*
*spent long winter months*

Just before you come to the hamlet, turn left along a pathway which runs between two low stone walls. At the edge of a beech wood, 500 metres further on, turn right onto a footpath leading down onto a path bordered by low walls. You come out onto the road just outside the village of Compains.

Take the D36 out of Compains in the direction of Brion. Just after the bridge, take a dirt track which turns off to the right at the corner of a house. Leave the track 20 metres further on, and turn left onto a path which winds up through a beech grove and comes out onto pasture. Leaving a farm, the Ferme de Malsagne, on your right 200 metres further on, you take the broad pathway to the left which leads southwards across pasture. It passes a shepherds' hut, the Buron de Barbe Sèche, and climbs the mountain of the same name. When you come to the D36, turn right along it in the direction of Brion. At the crossroads just outside the hamlet, turn right to the market place.

You leave the road and pass between two buildings where the GR30 and the GR41 separate. The GR41 carries straight on and the GR30 turns right behind the building. The GR30 follows a track which leads across a meadow, parallel to an electricity cable, to a shepherds' hut, the Burons de la Garde. Near the hut, you bear right towards a plantation. Carry on through the plantation and follow the path down into a small valley where it fords a stream and then climbs up to the D32. Here you turn right and follow the road to La Godivelle.

You carry on up into the village of La Godivelle until you come to the church.

**Lac d'en-Bas and Lac d'en-Haut**

La Godivelle lies between two very different lakes. Lac d'en-Bas is a peat bog lake in a shallow depression that the volcano containing the Lac d'en-Haut helped to close. It is now a nature reserve, visited by many nesting birds such as grebe, water rail and golden harrier, and migratory species such as the seagull, grebe, heron, stork, crane, cormorant and duck. Lac d'en-Haut is in a crater surrounded by reddish solidified volcanic cinder. Its clear waters reach a depth of 40m. Its steep shores indicate that, like Lac Pavin, it occupies an explosion crater. It is fed only by rainwater or the melting snows which flow down the sides of the crater. It is frozen over for weeks at a time, and in March 1889 the layer of ice reached a depth of 42cm.

**4Km**
**1:10**

*imprisoned in their thatched cottages, often cut off from the nearest hamlets for days at a time. The region well deserves the title 'Siberia of the Upper Auvergne'! The snow lies for 4 or sometimes 6 months in certain areas.*

You pass the church square, the fountain and the café on your left and leave the market town after a right-hand bend, to continue to the Lac de la Godivelle d'en-Haut. Carry on along the broad gravel track which climbs north-west, past the 1258-metre mark.

**Detour** *10 mins*
**Cross on the Montagne de Janson**
*There is a panoramic view across the lake, and the village of La Godivelle, the Monts du Cézallier and Le Cantal.*

The path leads gradually down to the Ferme de Gaine, and then on to the hamlet of Sandalouze. You continue along a lane, turning right and then left, and come to the church and square in the village of Espinchal.

**ESPINCHAL**
🏠 ⛺ ✕ ⚓
*1,052 m*

**7Km**
**2**

Go past the church and the school in Espinchal and take a broad, tree-lined pathway. When you come to the junction known as the Croix du Marquis, (Cross of the Marquis) take the path on the left and, 100 metres further on, go down across a meadow, across a stream, the Riochaux, where the path is muddy, and up the slope opposite. You bear slightly left and come to a pathway bordered by large stones leading off to the right to the hamlet of Redondel. Go through the hamlet and take a track suitable for motor vehicles. Follow this for 50 metres before bearing left along a sunken pathway leading up through pasture. Continue in a north-north-westerly direction until you come to the Ferme de la Clide. Soon afterwards, you go down to the right to the hamlet of Les Angles. Here, the GR turns right, passing near a stone cross, follows the edge of a beech grove and crosses a

stream above a waterfall, the Cascade du Boi de Chaux. It runs along the edge of the campsite of Egliseneuve and then beside a waterfall, La Cascade d'Entraigues. After crossing the River Clamouze, you come out onto the D978 which you follow to the left to Egliseneuve-d'Entraigues.

## EGLISENEUVE-D'ENTRAIGUES
🏠 ⌂ ✕ 🍷 ⚖
*955 m*
*Maison des Fromages d'Auvergne (Auvergne cheese centre)*

4Km
1:15

The GR4 from the direction of Lac Chauvet joins the GR30 and shares the same route as far as the Ferme d'Auger. At the junction of the D978 and the D30 in the village of Egliseneuve-d'Entraigues, turn right along the D30 for 50 metres and then turn left onto a fairly broad pathway leading up onto the plateau. At the Ferme d'Auger, the GR4 turns off to the left, and the GR30 carries straight on along a pathway bordered by beech trees. This brings you out onto the D30E near Les Aveix. Turn left along the D30E until you come to the Ferme des Chirouzes.

## Ferme des Chirouzes
*(map ref 16)*
*1,052 m*
**Detour** *10 mins*
## Lac de l'Esclauze
*The entire surface of this shallow lake is covered with sedge, water lilies and bulrushes. It is of great interest to naturalists and botanists. To the west of the lake, is an old crystalline platform marked by the effects of glaciation. It is an area of amazingly tortured rolling hills, lakes, peat bogs and marshy pastures, where cattle now graze.*
**Detour** *10 mins*
*The artificial reservoir of*
**Chabrol**
*Follow the D88 to the left.*

5Km
1:15

When you are on a level with a transformer, 100 metres before the Ferme des Chirouzes, turn right onto an old path which leads across the meadow and slopes gently down to a stream, the Gabacut. Cross the stream by the footbridge and turn left along the bank for 700 metres. You then follow a low wall up and onto a little road. NB: Make sure that you close the gates securely on this section of the route. Carry straight on along the pathway opposite leading to the farms of Lamadeuf, where the GR30 continues down to the D88.

The GR30 crosses the D88 and follows the lane leading to the hamlet of Chabrol.

## Chabrol
*990 m*

Just before the hamlet of Chabrol, the GR30 bears right along a pathway which comes to a stream, the Tauron. Follow the left bank of the stream and, just before you get to a barn, bear left into a wood, the Bois de Tenezeyre. You move away from the stream a little, crossing it further on by way of a wooden bridge. The

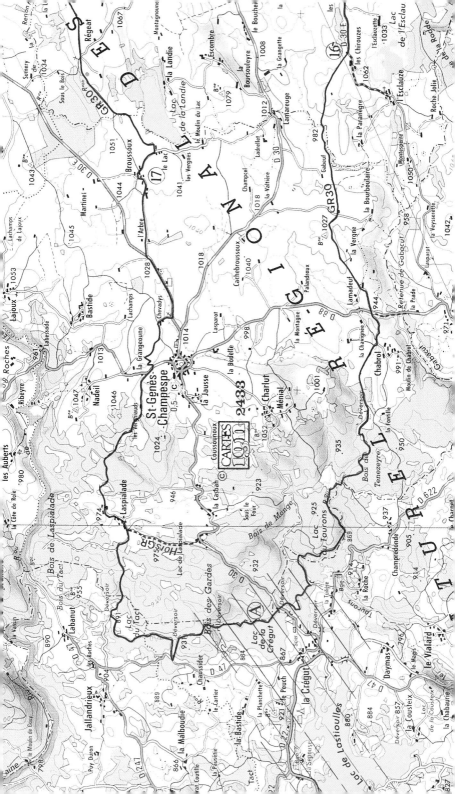

**Lac de la Crégut**
Formed by a pronounced 'over-hollowing' by glaciation of the rocks of the old crystalline platform, to a depth of 26m. The lakes further east were formed by surface hollowing of volcanic lava flows. Lac de la Crégut has been integrated into a hydraulic system of the 'Electricité de France'. There are important reservoirs further west.

5.5Km
1:30

GR30 continues along the edge of a meadow, the Tauron, and after crossing a little tributary, follows its right bank as far as the artificial reservoir of the Taurons. Turn right and follow the shore, crossing the marshy area at the northern end of the reservoir with care. You come out onto a gravel track which you follow for 200 metres and then turn right to the artificial reservoir of La Crégut. You cross the D30 and come to the Lac de la Crégut.

**LAC DE LA CRÉGUT**
▲ ✕ ♈
*(A on map)*
*875 m*

Follow the shore of the natural lake of La Grégut as you climb northwards to the edge of a wood, the Bois des Gardes. At the northern end of the lake, the GR30 follows a footpath which climbs steeply into the Bois des Gardes along the southern bank of a little stream. Follow a farm track for several metres which bears left and then right through the trees and brings you to another path leading down to the artificial reservoir. Turn right and follow its eastern shore until you come to the far end of the Lac du Tact. Turn right onto a pathway which runs through the Bois des Gardes from west to east and brings you to the hamlet of Laspialade.

7Km
2

**Detour** *30 mins*
**To Lac de Lespialade**
*A small lake, the result of 'over-hollowing' by glaciation, 12m deep, and surrounded by peat bogs. Trout from here are considered inedible because of their resinous taste.*

The GR30 goes through the hamlet of Laspialade, follows a sunken pathway and then turns right onto a footpath, bordered by high walls, leading through a beech forest. It passes through the Ferme des Vergniauds, and comes out onto the D88, about 300 metres from the market town of Saint-Genès-Champespe.

**SAINT-GENÈS-CHAMPESPE**
🏠 ⌂ ✕ ♨
*1,014 m*

Just outside Saint-Genès-Champespe, the GR30 turns right along the D88 for 50 metres and then left onto an area of common land. It follows a wall across a marshy area and takes

4Km
1

Le Lac
(map ref 17)
1,040 m
Situated to the northwest of
the Lac de la Landie. To the
east of Saint-Champespe,
the GR30 comes to the
volcanic lava flows of the
massif formed by the Monts
Dore.

7.5Km
2

the path leading to the Ferme des Chevadys. Passing behind the farm, it follows a pathway bordered by spruce and comes out on the D30E. Turn left along the D30E for 1 kilometre, and then bear right along a lane leading to the hamlets of Les Broussoux and Le Lac.

As you come to the hamlet of Le Lac, there is a farm on your right. You cross a grassy area bordered by bushes opposite the farm and continue along a pathway, bordered by very old trees and old walls, which is often muddy. The path follows the ridges, offering extensive views across to the Massif du Sancy in the north and the Massif du Cantal in the south. After a gentle climb, it runs above the Lac de la Landie and brings you out amongst the ruins of the old village of Régéat where you will see some very fine basalt walls. Carry straight on along the path which comes out of the wood onto a grassy area and continues along the ridge until it comes to the end of a little road near a farm. Carry on along the pathway opposite which runs eastwards. It disappears now and again as it crosses meadows and pasture, but follows the same direction until it bears left and crosses the D128, about 200 metres to the northwest of the hamlet of

## Lac de la Landie and Lac Chauvet

The Lac de la Landie lies in a depression formed by glacial erosion during the Quaternary Period. Fed by a stream its clear, cold waters rest on a bed of basalt rock. A peat bog has developed where the stream enters the lake, and at the overflow point at the southwestern corner, there is a much larger peat bog, the surface of which is at least 1m higher than the surface of the lake, suggesting that the water level has dropped considerably. A beautiful bank of water lilies has developed on the lake opposite the peat bog near the overflow, and there is a lush vegetation of aquatic plants at the point where the stream leaves the lake. Lac Chauvet, less severe in appearance than Lac Pavin, is similar in that it fills a large explosion crater, reaching a depth of 63m. Its gently sloping shores rise to the main crater, hidden beneath a forest of old beech trees. Previously, the lake was enclosed by the Bois-Noir and the Bois de Montbert, but forest clearance has opened up nearly half the circumference of the cirque. The surface has opened up nearly half the circumference of the cirque. The surface of the lake sometimes remains frozen over for months, thawing as late as the beginning of May. It is used for fish farming, particularly trout-breeding.

The watershed between the River Dordogne and the River Allier lies very close to Lac Chauvet. A breach of a few metres opened up in the Col de Vassivière would be enough to divert the two rivers, the Clamouze and the Couze de Pavin, from their natural courses into another river basin.

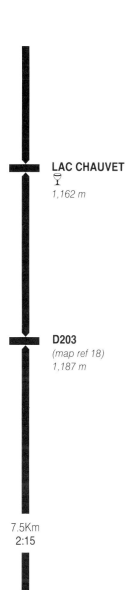

**LAC CHAUVET**
🍷
*1,162 m*

**D203**
*(map ref 18)*
*1,187 m*

7.5Km
2:15

Renonfeyre. The GR30 runs across the pasture of the Montagne de Mouillat, where the path becomes difficult to see. You bear left, northwards, to the hamlet of La Chaux where you turn right along a lane and then turn off to the right along a sunken pathway which follows the edge of a forest, the Forêt de Montbert, and comes out at Lac Chauvet.

When it comes to the refreshment stall at the north-west corner of Lac Chauvet, the GR climbs gently southwards into a forest, the Forêt de Montbert. It leaves the shore of the lake at its southern end, turning eastwards out of the forest. On the edge of the forest, the GR4 joins the GR30 from the right, from the direction of Egliseneuve-d'Entraigues. At the junction of the GR30 and the GR4 on the edge of the forest, turn left, and follow the path northwards along a ridge. You pass a shepherds' hut on your right and come to the D203.

This section of the GR30 runs mainly across the basalt lava flows of the massif of the Monts Dore. Turn right along the D203 for 100 metres and then bear left when you come to a fork. At the next intersection, the GR4 leaves the GR30, turning off to the right towards Super-Besse. The GR30 turns left along a little road and left again after 500 metres onto a grassy pathway leading along the edge of a coniferous plantation. When you come to a waterfall, the Cascade de la Barthe, on your left, skirt round it and follow the traces of a path which runs to the left along the edge of a beech grove. You cross a stream, the Escudor, and continue through pàsture as far as Le Cros, using the stepladders to cross the fences. Bear right behind the farm and cross the meadow, keeping to the left of the stream where the bank is marshy. At the top of the meadow, go towards the pines and then follow a low stone wall. Cross another low wall and continue to the right. When you come to a fence, follow it upwards to the left for 500 metres and then turn left along a pathway running through conifers which is a cross-country ski route. Follow it for 300 metres until you come to an intersection in the wood, the Bois de Gayme.

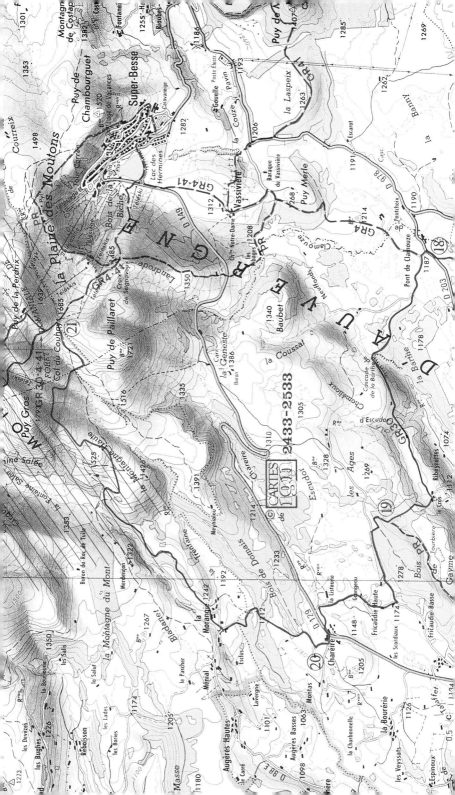

Intersection in the
**Bois de Gayme**
*(map ref 19)*
*1,250 m*
**Detour** *30 mins*
**PICHERANDE**
3Km
0:45
*1,120 m*
*Follow the PR route to the*
*left, marked with a dotted*
*line on the map.*

**CHAREIRE**
*(map ref 20)*
*1,180 m*

8Km
2:45

At the intersection the GR30 turns right along a grassy walk which comes out onto the road from Les Ages to Picherande. Turn left and follow it for 1 kilometre. When you come to Fricaudie-Haute, turn right past two farms. After Grangéou, continue along a dirt track which takes you through private property, so make sure you keep to the stepladders. Leaving La Listourne on your right, continue along a little road for 200 metres before turning left to Chareire.

In Chareire, turn right onto the road to Montas. You then turn right and right again, and come to the edge of a wood, the Bois de Domais. Take a path leading down and across a clearing and then back into the trees. At a junction of forest paths, take the one leading straight ahead to the bridge over the River Tarentaine. You go past a farm and then cross the road. Turn off it to the right just before the bridge, and climb up behind the hamlet of La Morangie. Take a broad pathway off to the left which leads up through a beech grove and comes out on the edge of the Vallée de la Fontaine Salée (Valley of the Salt Spring).

The GR30 winds upwards to the Montagne Haute. When you come to a fence, turn north-eastwards across a mass of fallen rocks to the foot of the Puy Gros. Turn right into a small valley and you soon come to a stream. Follow a fence for 50 metres, cross it and take the footpath leading along the side of the Puy de Paillaret to the Col de Couhay.

**Vallée de la Fontaine Salée**
This valley, like those of Le Mont-Dore and Chaudefour, was hollowed out by glaciation during the Quaternary Period. But, unlike them, it is not a conservation area, and is under serious threat from land developers. The site, named after the many mineral springs which rise there, is very unusual, and is of great educational and ecological interest. Its flora is remarkable due to the isolation, orientation and high level of humidity of the valley, and many original plant communities have remained intact. There are groves of beech and willow, and a whole range of associated plants such as the scilla, lily, hyacinth and woodrush. It has a rich and varied fauna. Bird life is specific to the altitude and includes rock thrushes, ring ouzels, alpine accentors and alpine pipits. The mammals are represented in particular by a large herd of mouflon. Aquatic life is that of high altitude streams and there are interesting examples of peatbog fauna and rare species of butterfly and beetle.

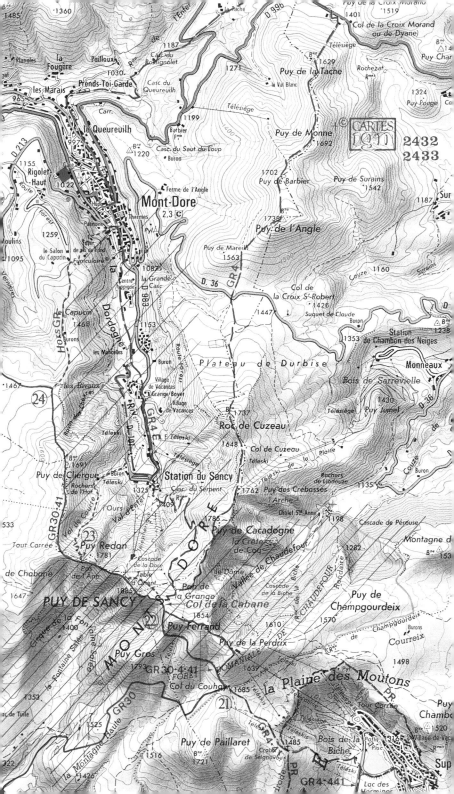

**Col de Couhay**
*(map ref 21)*
*1,685 m*
**Detour** *(GR4) 30 mins*
**SUPER-BESSE**
🏠 ⛺ 🍴 🍷 🚉
🚌
*(1,316 m*

2Km
0:30

**Col de la Cabane**
*(map ref 22)*
*1,770 m*
*Here, the GR30 leaves the*
*GR4 and the GR4E.*
**Detours** *(GR4E)*
*you can reach:*
*45 mins*
**STATION DU SANCY**
*(ski resort)*
🏠
*1,325 m*
**LE MONT-DORE**
🏠 ⛺ 🍴 🍷 🚉
🚂 🚌 🎫
*1,050 m*
*(Route marked with a dotted*
*line on the map.)*

1Km
0:20

**Puy de Sancy**
*1,885 m*

**Detour** *300 m*
*Cable-car from*
**LE MONT-DORE**
🍴

1Km
0:15

*Pass below the*
**Puy de Redon**
*(map ref 23)*
*1,722 m*
**Detour** *45 mins*
**STATION DU SANCY**
🏠
*(ski resort)*
*1,325 m*
*Follow the Val de Courre*
*down to the right.*

2.5Km
0:45

At the Col de Couhay, there are two possible routes. You can follow the path along the southern slopes of the Puy de la Perdrix and the Puy Ferrand, with the Puy Gros and the Vallée de la Fontaine Salée on your left, and come out on the Col de la Cabane (map ref 22). Alternatively, you can turn sharply northwards to the summit of the Puy de la Perdrix, where there is a cable-car station. Follow the watershed to the Puy Ferrand, from where there is a view across the Vallée de Chaudefour, and come down onto the Col.

From the Col de la Cabane, you can avoid climbing the Puy de Sancy by skirting round its base to the Pas de l'Ane. The GR30 winds up to the summit of the Puy de Sancy.

The GR30 comes down to the Pas de l'Ane.

From the Pas de l'Ane, take the footpath which leads off to the left along the ridge between the Vallée de la Fontaine Salée and the Vallée du Mont-Dore. You come to a pass below the Puy de Redon.

When you come to the Tour Carrée near the Puy de Chabanne, bear due north and follow the ridge along the edge of the Vallée du Mont-Dore. You pass via the Puy de Cliergue and continue down for 1 kilometre until you come to some copses and a junction of footpaths.

**Junction of footpaths**
*(map ref 24)*
*1,480 m*
**Detour** *45 mins*
**LE MONT-DORE**
🏠 ⛺ 🍴 🍷 🚠
🚌 🚃 🛈
*1,050 m*
*Take the footpath opposite*
*which leads downwards via*
*Le Capucin and Le Salon du*
*Capucin.*

7Km
2

At the junction of footpaths the GR30 bears left (west) along a track which climbs the Montagne de Bozat. You come to a fence. Between this point and the D213, the GR crosses private property. Right of way has been granted to walkers only. Make sure you follow the GR markings and close the gates, paying particular attention to livestock in summer. The existing buildings are in a very poor state of repair and may not be used as shelters. The continuation of the right of way depends upon the strict observance of these conditions,

Climb over the fence and follow the footpath which leads downwards, past a shepherds' hut, and comes to the edge of a forest. Go through the kissing gate and then follow the private road through the forest towards the D213.
Just before you reach it, take the pathway off to the right, leaving it after 100 metres to turn left onto a footpath which passes near a reservoir, climbs back up into the forest, and then crosses the road on the Plateau de Chamablanc. Carry straight on along the pathway opposite and then bear right 20 metres further on. You pass a barn and, after a short descent and a bend, you leave the pathway and take the footpath opposite leading down to Gibeaudet.

**GIBEAUDET**

⌂

*(map ref 25)*

**Detour** *45 mins*

1.5Km
0:20 **CENTRE OF LA BOURBOULE**

*Take the path leading down to Le Prégnoux.*

**D130**

Ⓐ

*(map ref 1)*

*855 m*

**LA BOURBOULE**

⌂ Ⓐ ✕ ⵛ ☎ ᴍᴍ

The GR30 turns right along the path leading down to a stream, the Vernières. Cross the stream by way of a footbridge and take the path off to the left which passes a chalet on a level with the access roads, the waterfalls, the Cascade de la Vernière and the Cascade du Plat à Barbe. From here you come to the D130, on the eastern side of La Bourboule.

# INDEX

The many different kinds of accommodation in France are explained in the introduction. Here we include a selection of hotels and other addresses, which is by no means exhaustive — the hotels listed are usually in the one-star or two-star categories. We have given full postal addresses so bookings can be made.

There has been an explosive growth in bed and breakfast facilities (chambers d'hôte) in the past few years, and staying in these private homes can be especially interesting and rewarding. Local shops and the town hall (mairie) can usually direct you to one.

Details of bus/train connections have been provided wherever it was possible. We suggest you refer also to the map inside the front cover.